FIRST STEPS IN
MESSIANIC
JEWISH
PRAYER

FIRST STEPS IN
MESSIANIC
JEWISH
PRAYER

AARON EBY

FIRST FRUITS OF
ZION

Copyright © 2014 First Fruits of Zion. All rights reserved.
Publication rights First Fruits of Zion, Inc.
Details: www.ffoz.org/copyright

Publisher grants permission to reference short quotations (less than 400 words) in reviews, magazines, newspapers, web sites, or other publications in accordance with the citation standards at www.ffoz.org/copyright. Requests for permission to reproduce more than 400 words can be made at www.ffoz.org/contact.

First Fruits of Zion is a 501(c)(3) registered nonprofit educational organization.

Printed in the United States of America

ISBN: 978-1-892124-90-6

The prayer text in this book, which includes Scriptural passages, is an original translation by the author.

All other Scriptural quotations, unless otherwise noted, are from the Holy Bible, English Standard Version®, copyright © 2001 by Crossway Bibles, a publishing ministry of Good News Publishers. Used by permission. All rights reserved.

Also cited: The New American Standard Bible®, © 1960, 1962, 1963, 1968, 1971, 1972, 1973, 1975, 1977, 1995 by The Lockman Foundation. Used by permission.

Cover design: Avner Wolff

Quantity discounts are available on bulk purchases of this book for educational, fundraising, or event purposes. Special versions or book excerpts to fit specific needs are available from First Fruits of Zion. For more information, contact www.ffoz.org/contact.

First Fruits of Zion

Israel / United States / Canada

PO Box 649, Marshfield, Missouri 65706–0649 USA
Phone (417) 468–2741, www.ffoz.org

Comments and questions: www.ffoz.org/contactt

CONTENTS

INTRODUCTION

ENTHRONED ON THE PRAISES OF ISRAEL

David declared of God, "You are holy, enthroned on the praises of Israel" (Psalm 22:4[3]). However, this verse comes in the midst of a psalm that describes a painful distance from God. The psalm opens with the words Yeshua uttered at the brink of death: "My God, my God, why have you forsaken me?" (Psalm 22:1).

The phrase "enthroned on the praises of Israel" seems strange in this context. Considering that this psalm reflects on such a troubling concept as the feeling of separation from God's presence, what does it mean by saying that God is "enthroned" on Israel's praises?

The prophets spoke about God's enthronement on earth. They foretold how the Messiah would usher in a time of peace, prosperity, and the revelation of God. This is the Messianic Kingdom.

Two thousand years ago, Yeshua of Nazareth came proclaiming that the kingdom was near and would be revealed if the people would turn their hearts to God in repentance. But if they would not, destruction would come. Because they did not repent, this kingdom was delayed, and the Jewish people experienced a time of exile lasting for millennia.

When Yeshua quoted Psalm 22, "My God, my God, why have you forsaken me?" he was not describing his personal feelings of anguish but prophetically announcing the departure of the Divine Presence and the onset of exile. God is the true King, but his kingship is currently concealed from this world. Instead, the world is dominated by materialism, corruption, and death.

Yeshua mobilized a revolutionary movement of people whose citizenship does not belong to this world but to the coming kingdom. We refuse to bow to the current world's regime; we stand strong and wait for our King to arrive—the God of Israel and his Messiah—and to reconquer what truly belongs to him.

At the core of this remnant is Israel; the "praises of Israel" found in the Siddur, or Jewish prayer book, today reflect the anticipation of God's official coronation here on earth. The day will soon come when, in the words of the *Aleinu* prayer,

> All humankind will call on your name, bringing all the wicked on earth to repentance. All of the world's inhabitants will recognize and know that every knee will bow and every tongue will swear allegiance to you. O LORD our God, they will bend their knees and fall before you, and they will glorify your precious name. They will all accept the yoke of your kingdom, and you will reign over them soon, forever and ever. For yours is the kingdom, and forever and ever you will reign with glory. As it is written in your Torah: "The LORD will reign forever and ever!"

In the meantime, we who submit ourselves to God's kingship constitute a resistance movement. Our fight is not against earthly nations and governments but the entire godless world system and the spiritual forces that hold sway.

Within our camps—our communities, our synagogues, and our homes—there is an enclave of Messianic Kingdom territory. And here God is enthroned; his throne exists in our midst as we sanctify his name. He is enthroned on the praises of Israel.

The early sages referred to one of the key components of Jewish prayer, the recitation of the *Shma,* as "accepting the yoke of the kingdom of heaven." It does not suffice to accept this yoke only once, but every single day we reaffirm our commitment and willingly subject ourselves to God's authority, whatever the cost.

We await the time when God's name is sanctified, his kingdom comes, and his will is done on earth as it is in heaven. In the meantime, we gather in our communities and in one voice make a collective pilgrimage to his heavenly throne room. There God meets with us, he strengthens us, he encourages us, he enlightens our eyes, and we bask in his Dwelling Presence.

Soon the day will come when the verses toward the end of Psalm 22 are also fulfilled:

> All the ends of the earth shall remember and turn to the LORD, and all the families of the nations shall worship before you. For kingship belongs to the LORD, and he rules over the nations. (Psalm 22:27–28)

MESSIANIC JEWISH PRAYER

This book is a brief introduction to prayer in Messianic Judaism. Jewish prayer is unique, both in its fundamental ideas and concepts and in the way it is practically observed.

In this book, we will examine the concepts of prayer from a Messianic Jewish perspective. Messianic Judaism is a type of Judaism. That means that the historical prayers of the synagogue across the centuries are our prayers. It was our sages, rabbis, poets, and prophets who penned these prayers and entrusted them to us, the Jewish community. Accordingly, this book will look at the aspects of prayer that we hold in common with all of Judaism. We will delve into the discussions of the scholars recorded in foundational, ancient Jewish works such as the Talmud and Midrash to see how they conceptualized prayer.

Messianic Judaism is a type of Judaism that is vitalized and enhanced by devotion to Yeshua (Jesus) of Nazareth as the Jewish Messiah. He taught us many things about how to pray. Messianic Judaism is especially equipped with the historical, cultural, and religious knowledge to understand and apply what he instructed about prayer. This book will focus on our Master Yeshua's brilliant, inspiring, and authoritative teachings on this topic as understood within their native Jewish context.

One important aspect of Jewish prayer that this book will explain is the daily prayer service. Each day at certain times, observant Jews pray a standard selection of prayers that has been cultivated and handed down over many centuries. In Messianic Judaism, it is common for Messianic Gentiles to participate in these prayers of Israel.

It is ideal to offer these prayers together in a prayer group called a *minyan*, whether at a synagogue or in a less formal setting. Even someone praying alone can offer these prayers and consider themselves joining the multitudes enthroning God throughout the world.

In this book, we will take a closer look at how the prayer services work and some of the main prayers that they contain. Specifically, we will look at six prayers with special significance to Messianic Judaism. These do not by any means constitute the complete corpus of daily Jewish prayer, but they at least give the reader a taste and an overview of prayer in Messianic Judaism.

This book presents the prayers in a similar way to what you will find in a Siddur, a traditional Jewish prayer book. Some readers may wish to use this book as an accessible starting point into Messianic Jewish prayer.

In order to keep this book as reader-friendly as possible, I have avoided burdening it with scholarly references. For a more exhaustive and detailed treatment of the topic, see the list of resources at the end of this book.

My prayer is that through this book, the name of the blessed Holy One would be glorified, praised, and revered. Let those who read it be encouraged to draw nearer to him with persistence, fervor, humility, and confidence. And let the greatness of his Son, our holy Master Yeshua the Messiah in whose merit and virtue we pray, be revealed to all.

PART 1

TEACHING ON PRAYER

PRAYER IN
MESSIANIC JUDAISM

I n Jewish interpretation prayer is a mitzvah, a duty incumbent
 on all humans, whether Jew or Gentile, man or woman, slave
or free. As with all mitzvot, prayer is beneficial to us; whether
our specific petitions are granted or not, we are rewarded for the
simple act of praying itself. Prayer is one way for us to store up
"treasures in heaven" (Matthew 6:20).

THE ESSENCE OF PRAYER

According to the sages, concentration in prayer is one of the deeds
for which one receives a reward in this world, and yet his principal
reward remains for him in the age to come.[1] Yeshua may have been
alluding to this when he remarked that people who are ostentatious in prayer "have received their reward" (Matthew 6:5). But
he assures us, "When you pray, go into your room and shut the
door and pray to your Father who is in secret. And your Father
who sees in secret will reward you" (Matthew 6:6).

The word "pray" in English fundamentally means "to ask" or
"to request." In Judaism we do make requests of God, but this is
only a part of what prayer means. To pray is to have an encounter
with God, to connect with him, and to commune with him. Prayer
is worthwhile and important whether we have personal requests
to make or not.

There are two main aspects of Jewish prayer: service and petition. "Service" in Hebrew is *avodah* (עֲבוֹדָה); this word connotes
the duties of the priests who ministered in the Tabernacle and in
the Temple. In our prayer we perform a labor on behalf of God.

Does God need our prayers? Similarly, did God need the sacrifices offered to him on the altar? Does he even benefit from them? Certainly God is lacking nothing, and there is nothing that we can offer him that he does not already have.

But God is not the beneficiary of our service; the world is. Through our prayers we transform ourselves and the world we live in. By opening the circuit between heaven and earth, we strengthen the connection between our own environment and God's presence. Serving God in prayer is preparing the way of HaShem in this world and straightening his path.

The word in Hebrew for "sacrifice" is *korban* (קָרְבָּן), which comes from a root meaning "to draw near." By serving God in prayer, we draw near to him, and that process sanctifies and purifies us. We come away from prayer changed and renewed.

Petitions and requests also represent an important component of prayer. Paul exhorted the Philippians, "Do not be anxious about anything, but in everything by prayer and supplication with thanksgiving let your requests be made known to God" (Philippians 4:6).

God often grants us what we ask. Yeshua instructed us to pray with faith and to trust that God would meet our needs. However, the purpose of petitioning God is not for us to get the things we want from God. In reality, sometimes we do not get what we ask for. In fact, both Moses and Yeshua made requests from God that were rejected; how much more will this sometimes be the case for us? But instead, our petitions serve as an acknowledgement that HaShem is the only one who can meet our needs. By placing our requests at his feet, we admit that despite our efforts and striving, he is the one who provides the result.

The Hebrew word for prayer is *tefillah* (תְּפִילָּה), which comes from the verb *lehitpalel* (לְהִתְפַּלֵּל). The literal meaning based on its root is "to judge oneself." This demonstrates the introspection and self-awareness that should accompany our approach to our Creator. We come as we are, laying aside any pretense or self-delusion. Yeshua taught us about the humble self-judgment that God favors in our praying in his parable about the Pharisee and the tax collector (Luke 18:11–14).

Ultimately, our prayers may or may not change our circumstances, but they are certain to change us. In Jewish prayer we not only lift our voices to God, but we hear him speak to us. We pray in the language of the Torah, the Prophets, and the Psalms; the words on our lips enter our own ears and pierce our hearts.

MANY FORMS OF PRAYER

Jewish prayer takes on many forms. One can pray alone, or one can join a congregation. Some prayer is said aloud, and sometimes it is only a whisper. Jewish prayers are often spoken in Hebrew, but they may be recited in any language one understands. Some Jewish prayers were composed thousands of years ago, whereas others are the simple outpouring of a person's heart.

Prayer is, at its core, communication with God, but different prayers serve different purposes as we communicate in different ways:

- A large congregation gathers in a grand synagogue, reciting ancient words in unison that rise to heaven as sacrificial offerings, enthroning God as King and affirming the covenant between Israel and her Redeemer.

- At home a mother lights her Sabbath candles and then quietly utters her deepest wishes for each of her children, knowing that God is near, attentive, and nurturing.

- A child holds a crisp, sweet apple and recites a formulaic blessing, acknowledging that his food comes from God.

- A woman sits beside the bed of an ill friend, intensely intonating the Psalms.

- A man finds a quiet place overlooking the sea and pours out his thoughts to his Abba in heaven in the way that he speaks to his best friend.

SERVICE OF THE HEART

In the ancient Temple the priests were required to perform many duties in connection with the sacrifices and offerings. These duties are collectively described in the Torah using the Hebrew word *avodah*, which, as we saw earlier, literally means "service" or "work."

But Scripture uses this term in another sense. Deuteronomy 10:12 reads,

> Now, Israel, what does the LORD your God require of you,
> but to fear the LORD your God, to walk in all his ways, to
> love him, to serve the LORD your God with all your heart
> and with all your soul.

What does it mean to serve God with one's heart? If "service" in the Temple means offering sacrifices, then what type of "service" would one do in his own heart?

The sages pondered this question and concluded that the phrase must be speaking of prayer.[2] Prayer is called the "service of the heart," or in Hebrew, *avodah shebalev* (עֲבוֹדָה שֶׁבַּלֵּב). This shows that a correlation exists between the priestly duties in the Temple and the communication of each person with God.

The core prayers found in the Siddur today originally accompanied the daily prayer services in the Temple. The daily times of prayer—evening, morning, and afternoon—correspond to different activities and services in the Temple. Commentators have noted that the structure of the prayers reflects a pilgrimage: going to the Temple, passing through its courts, entering the holy of holies, and finally exiting, step by step.

When the Temple was destroyed and the sacrificial services could no longer be performed, the sages explained that the prayers could continue nonetheless. They based this on Hosea 14:3[2]:

> Take words with you, and return to the LORD. Say to
> him, "Forgive all iniquity, and accept what is good. Let
> us exchange bulls for our lips." (Author's translation)

The Hebrew of this passage is difficult but clever. The word for "exchange" sounds as if it means "bring a peace offering." The word "bulls" is similar to the word "fruit," making a phrase reminiscent of "the fruit of our lips."

Hosea is appealing to Israel at the time when the northern kingdom had fallen into apostasy and were worshiping false gods. Their sacrifices to God were meaningless because of their unfaithfulness.

Hosea explains that the solution was not to offer more empty sacrifices. Rather, he says, "I desire covenant devotion rather than sacrifices, and the knowledge of God more than burnt offerings" (Hosea 6:6, author's translation). Hosea's desire was for the people to repent by turning to God with prayer and changing their ways.

The concept also applies in our time, while the Temple remains destroyed and sacrifices have ceased. Prayer, repentance, and good deeds are the key to seeing Israel restored and redeemed.

The author of Hebrews also picks up on this theme, comparing words and good deeds to sacrificial offerings:

> Through him then let us continually offer up a sacrifice of praise to God, that is, the fruit of lips that acknowledge his name. Do not neglect to do good and to share what you have, for such sacrifices are pleasing to God. (Hebrews 13:15–16)

THE ROLE OF YESHUA IN OUR PRAYERS

Yeshua taught us to address our prayers to the Father. He told us to pray like this: "Our Father, who is in heaven, let your name be sanctified" (Matthew 6:9, author's translation). He also instructed, "In that day you will ask nothing of me. Truly, truly, I say to you, whatever you ask of the Father in my name, he will give it to you." (John 16:23).

MEDIATOR OR INTERMEDIARY?

In Messianic Judaism we consider Yeshua to be a mediator in prayer. But in what sense? And is this truly a Jewish concept? Anti-missionaries, those who oppose Christian efforts to evangelize Jews, often object that Jews do not need an intermediary. They say, "We can pray to God directly."

Their objections are valid; we can indeed pray to God directly. However, there is a big difference between a mediator and an intermediary. A mediator is one who brings two parties together, reconciling the two and eliminating the distance and barriers between them. An intermediary, on the other hand, is a go-between.

When an intermediary is present, the two parties remain separate and only speak through the third party.

Yeshua is a mediator, not an intermediary. His righteous life, sacrificial death, and post-resurrection intercession on our behalf pave the way for us to have direct access to God our Father with no barriers and no person in our way.

In 1 John 2:1 Yeshua is called our "advocate," which in Greek is *parakletos* (παράκλητος). This Greek word became a loan word in Mishnaic Hebrew: *praklit* (פְּרַקְלִיט), which is used in a similar way. An ancient commentary on Leviticus uses this word to explain why a sin offering must be brought before bringing a burnt offering. It compares it to a person who wishes to bring a gift to the king:

> A sin offering can be compared to a *praklit*, who enters [the king's palace] to find favor. Once the *praklit* has gained [the king's] favor, the gift [i.e., the burnt offering] may be presented.[3]

The *praklit* is able to find favor with the king because of his own standing and merit, which he then uses to provide the petitioner direct access to the king.

IN YESHUA'S NAME

But what does it mean to ask the Father "in Yeshua's name?" The idiom "in the name of," in Hebrew (*beshem*, בְּשֵׁם), means "as a representative of," or "on the authority of." If we ask God for something in Yeshua's name, we are asking him to respond to us because of our association with Yeshua. In a way, we are merely the messenger; the request truly belongs to him. When we ask in Yeshua's name, it is not as though Yeshua is pleading on our behalf; rather, we are pleading on his behalf:

> In that day you will ask in my name, and I do not say to you that I will ask the Father on your behalf; for the Father himself loves you, because you have loved me and have believed that I came from God. (John 16:26–27)

It is a little bit like a person who is given a company credit card. He makes purchases on behalf of the company because he has been delegated the authority to do so. The payment, as large as it may be, can be made because it is drawn on the company credit card.

This implies two things. First, the petitions on our lips are accepted by God due to the merit and virtue of Yeshua—not our own. Second, asking in Yeshua's name is not a license to name and claim whatever we like. Instead, we only have license to ask for things that pertain to our capacity as Yeshua's agents in the world, and whatever we do receive in his name ultimately belongs to him and not to us.

This is what it means to pray in Yeshua's name. It does not require saying the words "in Yeshua's name" as a magic formula or that every prayer must end with "in Yeshua's name, amen." On the other hand, it is quite common in Judaism to include legal formalities when praying, and thus it is perfectly appropriate to mention Yeshua and to request that our prayers be answered on his behalf.

THE TZADDIK

Surely God was accessible and answered prayers before Yeshua came. This raises questions about how Yeshua benefits us as a mediator and why it is necessary for us to ask for things in his name.

Psalm 145:18–19 promises,

> The LORD is near to all who call on him, to all who call on him in truth. He fulfills the desire of those who fear him; he also hears their cry and saves them.

Furthermore, we can see examples of individuals who called upon God and were answered. Elijah is just such an example: his prayers stopped and started the rain. Was Yeshua his mediator?

These examples notwithstanding, we know from experience and history that Scriptures such as these describe an ideal principle rather than an inviolable law of the cosmos. It often happens that individuals pray but do not receive the answer they desire.

Rabbinic literature describes how, in times of distress, the sages of Israel would seek out individuals whose prayers were frequently answered:

Once it happened that the son of Rabban Gamliel became sick. He sent two scholars to Rabbi Chanina ben Dosa to pray for mercy on his behalf. When he saw them, he went to the upper room and prayed for mercy on his behalf. When he came back down, he told them, "Go; the fever has left him." They asked him, "How would you know that? Are you a prophet?" He told them, "I am not a prophet, nor am I the son of a prophet, but this is what I have learned: If my prayer is smooth in my mouth, I know that it is accepted, but if not, I know that it is denied." They sat down and took note of the exact moment when this happened. When they returned to Rabban Gamliel, he told them, "I swear that you have not added or subtracted a single moment! That was the very time that the fever left him and he asked us for water to drink."[4]

This is only one of numerous accounts of healings and miracles performed by Rabbi Chanina ben Dosa and a few other individuals like him. A student of the Gospels cannot help but notice the similarity these stories bear to events that took place during Yeshua's life.

Passages like this raise a few questions. Why did Rabban Gamliel have to send scholars to Rabbi Chanina ben Dosa? Couldn't Rabban Gamliel have prayed on his own? Couldn't the two scholars have prayed and received an answer for themselves?

They recognized that there was something unique about Rabbi Chanina. His prayers were frequently answered because he was a *tzaddik* (צַדִּיק), an exceptionally righteous individual. Though he was human like everyone else, Rabbi Chanina had merit and standing before God that most people did not. The same goes for individuals in the Bible like Elijah.

This is why people naturally turn to righteous individuals for prayer. Moses was able to gain forgiveness for the Israelites who sinned because he found favor with God (Exodus 33:17). The people turned to the Prophet Jeremiah to ask for prayer after Ishmael killed Gedaliah (Jeremiah 42:1–4). The people turned to Samuel to ask him to pray for them for the sin of asking for a king (1 Samuel 12:19).

This concept is attested in the New Testament. James teaches us,

> Confess your sins to one another and pray for one another, that you may be healed. The prayer of a righteous person [i.e., a tzaddik] has great power as it is working. Elijah was a man with a nature like ours, and he prayed fervently that it might not rain, and for three years and six months it did not rain on the earth. Then he prayed again, and heaven gave rain, and the earth bore its fruit. (James 5:16–18)

The ancient sages echoed this idea and provided a source from the Hebrew Scriptures:

> Rav Pinchas bar Chama expounded: Anyone who has a sickness in his household should go to a sage that he may pray for mercy. As it is said, "A king's wrath is a messenger [i.e., an angel] of death, and a wise man [i.e., a sage] will appease it." (Proverbs 16:14)[5]

Many centuries after this was written, the tzaddik concept flourished in Chasidic Judaism. Dov Ber (the "Maggid") of Mezeritch was the chief disciple of Rabbi Israel Baal Shem Tov and one of the founders of Chasidic Judaism. Paul Philip Levertoff summarized Dov Ber's views this way:

> The tzaddik is the pet or favorite of heaven, the instrument through which God sends his grace into the world. Through his communion with God, he is the connection between God and creation, and as such, he is the bearer and mediator of blessing and grace. The love that man has for the tzaddik is therefore the means through which God's grace is won. The duty of every Chasid is this: that he loves the tzaddik and listens to his word.[6]

Understood this way, Yeshua is the ultimate tzaddik. He has earned merit and favor before God that not even Elijah or Rabbi Chanina achieved. It is not as though our prayers would not be heard by God on our own, but rather, would he have a good reason to answer them? By clinging to Yeshua—that is, by identifying with him, following him, and trusting in him—we benefit from his merit, and God answers our prayers on his account.

However, it bears repeating that we do not bring our requests to Yeshua so that he may in turn relay them to our heavenly Father, as the scholars did with Rabbi Chanina. Rather, his merit benefits us directly, because when we pray to God, we do so as disciples of Yeshua.

Although as individuals we are faulty and undeserving, God accords us the honor due to a tzaddik because we stand before him in the capacity of Yeshua's official representatives. And just as God shows such favor to us, we too should treat fellow disciples as bearing the merit of Yeshua, even if they do not deserve it in and of themselves.

PRAYER IN JEWISH SPACE

Rituals, including prayer, have the potential to enhance and elevate a person spiritually. They can bring discipline and rhythm to one's life, and they can serve as a way to worship God in a beautiful and holy way. They can provide consistency in one's life and unity between individuals, families, communities, and generations.

KAVANAH

And yet with rituals there is always a danger that a person may become desensitized to their meaning or distracted in doing them. Rather than engaging in the activity with full consciousness, concentration, and enthusiasm, a person may simply go through the motions but not truly connect with the Creator in a meaningful way.

Jewish teaching deems it necessary that we have proper mental focus during prayer and other rituals. One must pause, think about what he or she is doing, and have appropriate mental concentration during the act. This type of focus or concentration during prayer is called by the Hebrew term *kavanah* (כַּוָּנָה). Numerous rabbis throughout the centuries have cautioned, "Prayer without *kavanah* is like a body without a soul."

One must focus on the meaning of a prayer, although that does not necessarily mean concentrating on the grammatical function of each syllable. Focusing on the general concept is the important thing. When praying, one must clear the mind from distractions and see himself as standing in the very presence of God.

WINDOWS OF OPPORTUNITY: PRAYER AT SET TIMES

One can pray at any time of the day. However, there are particular times every day when the Jewish community across the world prays collectively.

At each of these times, individuals recite the appropriate prayer service from the prayer book. A prayer service is a selection of prayers from the Siddur that have been compiled and assigned to a particular time of prayer—morning, afternoon, or evening.

Orthodox synagogues have congregational services at each of these times every day. Ad-hoc prayer groups (minyans) are also often formed wherever ten Jewish men happen to be at the time.

These times of prayer correspond with times when certain sacrifices were offered in the Temple.

The Torah ordains that there should be two lambs offered as a burnt offering each weekday. One of the lambs is to be offered in the morning and the other in the afternoon. They are the first and last sacrifices that are brought throughout the day; all the other weekly sacrifices are sandwiched between them.

These two offerings are called the *korban tamid* (קָרְבַּן תָּמִיד), which means "continual offering." On Sabbaths and holidays additional burnt offerings are brought. These are referred to as the *korban mussaf* (קָרְבַּן מוּסָף), which means "additional offering." These offerings are described in Numbers 28:

> Command the people of Israel and say to them, "My offering, my food for my food offerings, my pleasing aroma, you shall be careful to offer to me at its appointed time." And you shall say to them, "This is the food offering that you shall offer to the LORD: two male lambs a year old without blemish, day by day, as a regular offering. The one lamb you shall offer in the morning, and the other lamb you shall offer at twilight." (Numbers 28:2–4)

Notice how this passage refers to the time of sacrifice as an "appointed time." The Hebrew word used here is *mo'ed* (מוֹעֵד). The same word is used to describe the festivals in Leviticus 23. Just as the holy festivals such as Passover, Shavu'ot, and Sukkot are special opportunities for us to meet with God, there are two *mo'adim*—times of appointment—with God each day.

The *Amidah* is the central prayer of each prayer service. While the Temple stood, this prayer was offered in sync with the burnt offerings. Now that sacrifices cannot be offered, the prayer is offered alone, without the sacrifice, at the time of the offerings.

There are three times for the prayer service each day:

- *Shacharit* (morning)
- *Minchah* (afternoon)
- *Ma'ariv* (evening)

The *shacharit* prayers correspond to the daily burnt offering in the morning. The *minchah* prayers correspond to the daily burnt offering in the afternoon. *Ma'ariv* does not correspond to a specific sacrifice, but it represents the burning of any leftovers from the sacrifices on the altar, which went on throughout the night. Leviticus 6:2[9] instructs,

> Command Aaron and his sons, saying, This is the law of the burnt offering. The burnt offering shall be on the hearth on the altar all night until the morning, and the fire of the altar shall be kept burning on it.

According to Jewish tradition, the prayer times actually predate the Temple sacrifices. Abraham, Isaac, and Jacob were men of prayer, and the Midrash connects the Torah's accounts of prayer with each of the prayer times.[7]

DETERMINING THE PROPER TIMES

There are rules that govern when the priests can offer each sacrifice at the altar. Since the times of prayer correspond to the sacrifices, these rules also govern the proper time for each prayer service.

There is not an exact moment when the prayers must be offered. Rather, there is a fairly large window of time for each prayer. This window is not based on modern timekeeping methods but on the position of the sun in the sky.

The morning sacrifice was not offered until sunrise, and it could be offered any time before the sun reached the middle of the sky—that is, around noon. This means that when praying in the morning, one should try to time it so that he does not reach the *Amidah* prayer before the sun comes up and does not finish the *Amidah* after midday. (Note that during daylight saving time in the summer, astronomical midday does not take place until about one o'clock.)

The earliest the afternoon sacrifice could be offered was a half hour after midday. As for the latest time it could be offered, there are two accepted opinions. According to one view, it had to be offered by sunset. According to another view, it was to be offered no later than one and a quarter hours before sunset, at a time called *plag haminchah* (פְּלַג הַמִּנְחָה).

These two views also differ regarding when the evening prayers could begin. According to the first opinion, which allowed the afternoon sacrifice to be offered until sunset, one could not begin the evening prayers until it became dark and the stars began to appear. This is typically about a half hour after sunset. According to the view that the afternoon offering had to be offered by an hour and a quarter before sunset, one can pray the evening prayers any time after that.

In practice both opinions are upheld. While one should not vacillate between one and the other, one can choose the view that is most convenient and stick with it for a while. For example, if you want to get the prayers done earlier, you can follow the early opinion. This works well especially when a group is gathered for prayer, because if they time things right, they can pray the two services back-to-back. If a person works late and finds it difficult to pray *minchah* until just before sunset, he can follow the late opinion.

Since the leftovers could burn all night until dawn, one technically has until dawn to recite the evening prayers. However, the sages decided that it would be ideal to finish them before astronomical midnight.

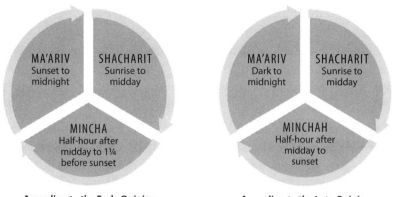

	MA'ARIV Sunset to midnight	SHACHARIT Sunrise to midday
	MINCHA Half-hour after midday to 1¼ before sunset	

According to the Early Opinion

	MA'ARIV Dark to midnight	SHACHARIT Sunrise to midday
	MINCHAH Half-hour after midday to sunset	

According to the Late Opinion

To help put these times in perspective, below is a table of what the times of prayer would look like on a "perfect day," when the sun rises at 6:00 a.m. and sets at 6:00 p.m., and the stars appear at 6:30. However, in reality such a day would rarely exist; the times fluctuate widely with the seasons.

	According to the Early Opinion	According to the Late Opinion
Shacharit	6:00 a.m. – noon	6:00 a.m. – noon
Minchah	12:30 p.m. – 4:45 p.m.	12:30 p.m. – 6:00 p.m.
Ma'ariv	4:45 p.m. – midnight	6:30 p.m. – midnight

On the Sabbath and on holidays, there is an additional recitation of the *Amidah*, corresponding to the additional burnt offering (the *korban mussaf*). There is no prescribed time for this prayer, but it is typically placed immediately after the *shacharit* service.

There seem to be allusions to these times of prayer in Scripture. King David wrote, "Evening and morning and at noon I utter my complaint and moan, and he hears my voice" (Psalm 55:18[17]). Daniel 6:10 explains, "When Daniel knew that the document had been signed, he went to his house where he had windows in his upper chamber open toward Jerusalem. He got down on his knees three times a day and prayed and gave thanks before his God, as he had done previously."

Times in the Jewish calendar are counted as hours from sunrise. The span of time between sunrise and sunset is divided into twelve equal portions. Each portion is considered an hour, even though the actual length of these portions will vary throughout the year. Note that each "hour" is not a moment on the clock but a segment of time that is one twelfth of the daylight.

In our "perfect day" scenario, the hours of the day would occur as follows:

First hour	6:00 – 7:00
Second hour	7:00 – 8:00
Third hour	8:00 – 9:00
Fourth hour	9:00 – 10:00
Fifth hour	10:00 – 11:00
Sixth hour	11:00 – 12:00
Seventh hour	12:00 – 1:00
Eighth hour	1:00 – 2:00
Ninth hour	2:00 – 3:00
Tenth hour	3:00 – 4:00
Eleventh hour	4:00 – 5:00
Twelfth hour	5:00 – 6:00

MESSIANIC SYMBOLISM IN THE TIMES OF PRAYER

The times of prayer are also mentioned in the New Testament. For example, the *shacharit* prayers are mentioned in Luke 1:10: "The whole multitude of the people were praying outside at the hour of incense." The early rabbis recalled that the burning of the incense took place after the blood of the morning *korban tamid* was splashed on the altar but immediately before it was burned.[8]

Our Master Yeshua prayed early in the morning (Mark 1:35). This seems to mesh with the custom of the ancient Chasidim, who would meditate an hour before prayer[9] and recite the *Amidah* exactly at sunrise.[10]

Acts 2:15 indicates that it was the third hour of the day, within the time for *shacharit*, when the multitude was gathered at the Temple on Shavu'ot.

It was the ninth hour of the day when Cornelius was praying, according to Acts 10:3. The hours are counted from sunrise. This means that Cornelius was praying in the afternoon, well within the prescribed time for *minchah*. In fact, Acts 3:1 refers to the ninth hour as "the hour of prayer," when Peter and John went up to the Temple.

As disciples of Yeshua, we cannot help but connect his own sacrifice of his life with the sacrificial offerings in the Temple. This is not only true of the Passover lamb—each of the Temple offerings relates to Yeshua in some way. That means that by praying in concert with the times of sacrifice, we are in a sense memorializing our Master Yeshua. The New Testament indicates that Yeshua's execution began at the third hour, the time of *shacharit* (Mark 15:25). He died at the ninth hour, the time of *minchah* (Matthew 27:46–50; Mark 15:34–37; Luke 23:44–46).

BY THE BOOK: PRAYING FROM A SCRIPT

Praying at certain times of the day might seem unpleasantly rigid to those who are unfamiliar with the practice. For people who come from a non-liturgical background, praying a scripted prayer may seem an even more foreign idea. Is it possible for us to mean what we are saying when our prayers are scripted?

It bears repeating that not all Jewish prayer is preformulated. On the other hand, there are many occasions when Judaism is quite comfortable with praying from a prewritten text. This was the case in the days of the apostles and for centuries before that.

The prayer that Yeshua taught his disciples, commonly referred to as the "Lord's Prayer," is just such an example of a pre-scripted Jewish prayer. Some denominations feel uncomfortable with using the prayer verbatim and prefer to see it as an outline. However, when looking at the context of first-century Judaism, it becomes clear that it was intended as a verbatim prayer. In that era it was quite common for rabbis to formulate prayers for their disciples and to discuss the appropriate formulation for certain prayers.

Early church literature shows that ancient believers recited the prayer verbatim as a part of liturgy.

VAIN REPETITIONS?

Yeshua condemned certain types of prayer. But did he have Jewish liturgy in sight? In Matthew 6:7 he says,

> When you pray, do not heap up empty phrases as the Gentiles do, for they think that they will be heard for their many words.

Note that Yeshua's criticism of such longwinded babbling was not directed at traditional Judaism or Pharisees. He specifically identified the culprits as Gentiles.

Although the term translated "heap up empty phrases" is sometimes translated "use vain repetitions," it refers to a mode of prayer that involved uttering a drawn-out stream of nonsense. This certainly does not describe the traditional Jewish mode of prayer. Instead, it is evocative of the prophets of Baal in the contest with Elijah:

> And as midday passed, they raved on until the time of the offering of the oblation, but there was no voice. No one answered; no one paid attention. (1 Kings 18:29)

LOSS OF MEANING?

Does praying the same prayer day after day lead to it losing meaning? This can sometimes be the case. A person can get stuck in the ritual of prayer and fail to focus on the meaning of the words and their potential to help him connect with God.

However, it might be just the opposite. Each time you a read a passage from the Scriptures, do you discover that it means more or less to you? If you are attentive, the passage will mean more to you each time you read it. The more often you read it, the less time it will take for you to recall what it means.

The same can be true of the prayers. The prayers are deeply poetic and profound. At first it can be difficult to focus on them and to understand them. But each time you pray, you may notice more and more about them, and it will become easier to concentrate on the meaning.

It is like a person who walks through a field or a forest. At first, trudging through the weeds is difficult and slow going, but after doing so day after day, week after week, and year after year, it becomes easier and easier to get from point A to point B.

Spontaneous prayers, like traditional prayers, are not immune to the threat of becoming meaningless or empty over time. Whether praying traditionally or spontaneously, a person who is praying must always pay special attention to his task and be intentional about seeking God in prayer.

QUENCHING THE SPIRIT?

Do pre-scripted prayers constrain the Holy Spirit? Some people feel that being inspired by the Holy Spirit means being spontaneous or unpredictable and avoiding a plan or a schedule. This is not necessarily the case.

Even charismatic Christian churches have a service that tends to follow a specific order. They sing songs and choruses and display the pre-scripted words on large screens. This is as much a type of liturgy as is the *Amidah* or the *Shma*.

The Holy Spirit can also inspire things that are structured and written. It was the Holy Spirit that filled the Tabernacle. And yet it pleased God to have a specific order and structure to the way the services were run. In fact, the Bible itself is inspired by the Holy Spirit, and the Bible is structured and written.

Sometimes people from a charismatic Christian background misunderstand the Hebrew idiom of "walking in the Spirit." This does not indicate an unplanned manner of life that relies on constant, unpredictable direction from God. Instead, it describes a life in which one subdues their fleshly, self-serving impulses in favor of carrying out every detail of God's commandments.

The ability to be spontaneous and adaptable at times is certainly a positive quality. And yet this is not incompatible with liturgy, nor is it synonymous with Holy Spirit inspiration. In fact, liturgical prayer can even be a springboard for spontaneity in prayer and can bring ideas to mind that one might not have thought of otherwise.

BEING PERSONAL IN PRAYER

Are the synagogue prayers too impersonal and detached from the individual? If synagogue liturgy were the sum of one's prayer life, it would seem tragically impersonal and distant. But Judaism draws a distinction between corporate and private prayer.

The synagogue liturgy is often not personal. That is by design. There are times when it is appropriate to focus on personal issues, but when we stand united with all Israel, our personal issues are miniscule compared to the glory of God and his kingdom. The point is to get our minds off ourselves.

NEGATIVE PAST EXPERIENCES

Some people's past experiences in liturgical settings, whether in Judaism or in Christianity, turn them off to praying in a liturgical way.

Someone who was raised with a liturgical tradition that he or she did not appreciate is presented with the difficult challenge of overcoming emotional barriers and looking at something with new eyes. That can be difficult, but it is worth it.

Some people find praying in a customary Jewish way to be energizing and spiritually moving. There are others who grew up in a free-flowing, spontaneous prayer-and-worship environment who have difficulty relating to liturgical prayer. They may not get the same positive feeling from it that they do with other forms of worship.

But prayer takes sacrifice and dedication. We do not worship or pray because we enjoy it, although that may often be the case. We worship because God deserves it. Everyone likes to feel spiritually charged, but whether or not a person feels spiritually charged from a form of worship should not be the primary issue. True worship is submission to God. Our goal should be to determine how God wants us to worship him.

CONNECTING WITH GOD, MESSIAH, OUR COMMUNITY, AND THE GENERATIONS

When people join together to accomplish the same goal, their united efforts tend to be much more successful than individual effort can be. This is true in the case of prayer.

People sometimes see prayer at fixed times or from a book as limiting or constraining, but in fact it is exactly the opposite. When we offer up the prayers of Israel at the appointed times of the day, whether we are with a congregation or alone, our voices join a chorus that spans the entire globe. Waves of prayer constantly circle the earth as it spins on its axis, and we have the opportunity to be a part of them each time they come our way.

This type of prayer forges unity not only with members of the commonwealth of Israel across the globe but also with the generations of Israel throughout the centuries. In a timeless way our voices mingle with those of the faithful remnant of God's people across the ages and even with the prayers of the early disciples and of Yeshua himself.

Liturgy remained a significant part of formal worship in the early community of believers, even after the community separated from Judaism. It is our heritage.

You probably have participated in corporate prayer before, which can sometimes be a thrilling and meaningful experience in which prayers are answered and God's presence is felt. But if the unity of thousands of worshipers gathered in a stadium for a single event is powerful, how much more is the unity of the nonstop prayer meeting that has been happening now for thousands of years!

As disciples of Yeshua, we have a special calling and ability to infuse in that wave of prayer the power of the name of the Messiah.

Of course, unity is more than just saying the same words at the same time. But the collection of prayers in the Siddur is a catalyst for unity. It is a way to centralize our thoughts and intentions and to agree together on certain things that are important. Some people are surprised to find that the prayers offer them the opportunity to pray about things that had never entered their mind before. When specific needs and petitions are brought to their mind, they are better able to identify and be united with all Israel.

EXPANDING OUR PERSPECTIVE

It is easy in prayer to focus on ourselves and on the little things. In corporate worship from the Siddur, we have a chance to widen our perspective. In addition to asking God to heal the sick people we know, we offer prayers that God would bring healing to the entire world. We ask that he would bring everlasting peace to the world. We ask that he would reign over all the world in his glory. We aim high in our corporate prayers, asking for the ultimate redemption, the coming of the Messiah, and the restoration of all things!

The prayers in the Siddur do not focus on us as individuals (although it allows some room for that at appropriate times). In this way it enables us better to focus on God, his plan, and his kingdom. The traditional Jewish liturgy offers us the benefit of expanding our perspective and helps us to focus on the larger picture in prayer.

PRAYER AS POETRY

It is not uncommon for people to find it difficult to pray because they just don't know what to say. Many people find that the words in the Siddur express their own heart eloquently and poetically. The scribes and scholars and lyricists who formulated these prayers clearly had a deep level of relationship with God. They knew the Hebrew Scriptures inside and out. They wove together blessings from the Torah, oracles from the Prophets, and petitions from the Psalms in a beautiful tapestry of prayer that is deeply poetic and extremely biblical.

The Siddur is a compilation of the most beloved prayers of Israel that have been penned over numerous centuries. Many followers of Yeshua who have a heart that is united with Israel find that these are the words that they have been grasping for.

PRAYER AS CONVERSATION

The traditional Jewish prayers are more than a simple monologue. Since they are saturated in Scripture, through them we are not only able to make our voice heard by God, but we can also hear him speaking to us through his word. Prayer is meant to be conversation, and conversation is meant to involve both speaking and listening.

For example, as we read the passages of the *Shma*, we recite phrases such as, "And these words, which I command you today, shall be on your heart." These are not our words; they are God's words to us. We are able to hear from God as he speaks to us through the Scriptures embedded in the prayers.

PRAYER AS MEDITATION AND STUDY

When a person prays the traditional Jewish prayers on a regular basis, it is not long before he has several extended passages of Scripture memorized. The Scriptures in the synagogue prayers are not all cut-and-pasted verses; there are many entire chapters and long sections that we read, chant, or sing on a constant basis. It is inevitable that a person who remains dedicated to the traditional prayers will have a lot of the Bible committed to memory before long—especially Psalms. If you hope to memorize more Scripture, this is a surefire way to do it.

FOCUS ON THE MESSIAH AND REDEMPTION

The traditional Jewish prayers are constantly focused on the Messiah. Although they do not identify Yeshua by name, they do identify the Messiah by character and by title.

Some people might object that the traditional Jewish prayers do not say anything about Yeshua since they do not mention him by name. The same is true of the Hebrew Scriptures, yet we know that they say a great deal about Yeshua.

Messianic prophecies and promises appear throughout the Siddur because the prayers are constantly looking toward the time of the ultimate redemption. As a result of this, it is very easy to remain centered on the Messiah during prayer.

PRAYER IN HEBREW

Most of the prayers in Judaism are written in Hebrew. Hebrew is considered the best language for prayer. It is the holy language and the tongue of angels. Hebrew is the language in which God spoke the world into being, revealed the Torah at Mount Sinai, and spoke through the prophets.

In Judaism a knowledge of Hebrew is not reserved for a class of elite scholars, as Greek tends to be for Christians. Rather, any Jewish person with a basic religious education has learned the fundamentals of Hebrew. This makes Scripture in its purest form, as well as the many classic texts of Judaism, available to a student. Conversely, failure to learn Hebrew can be the first step in a path to assimilation from firm Jewish identity into secular society.

There are many benefits to praying in Hebrew:

- A common, shared language brings about unity among congregations spanning the world and the generations. "For at that time I will change the speech of the peoples to a pure speech, that all of them may call upon the name of the LORD and serve him with one accord" (Zephaniah 3:9). It is an amazing thing to think that our Hebrew prayers would be understood by Yeshua and his disciples, by King David, by Moses, or by Abraham!

- Reciting daily prayers and readings in Hebrew helps a person learn and memorize Scripture in its original language.

- Familiarity with prayers and songs in Hebrew reinforces Jewish identity and literacy, which is essential in Messianic Jewish communities.

- Knowing Hebrew can help a person more accurately understand the original sense of the prayers and Scripture passages without filtering it through a translation. It also enables a person to see and appreciate the poetry and artistic nuances in the text that cannot be translated.

On the other hand, prayer requires *kavanah*, and the most basic requirement of *kavanah* is understanding what we are saying. If a person does not know Hebrew, then how can he or she pray in Hebrew with *kavanah*?

The Jewish sages conclude that an individual may pray in any language one understands if he does not understand Hebrew. For this reason many Siddurim have a side-by-side translation in the local vernacular, which allows individuals to pray in their mother tongue while the prayer leader prays in Hebrew.

Some people may not be able to understand Hebrew but can sound out Hebrew words or read from a transliteration. This is acceptable, but one must then be sure to read or learn the English translation first and then concentrate on the meaning of the prayer when reciting it.

Ultimately, it is important for individuals to pursue mastery of the Hebrew language the best they are able.

Prayer in a Congregation

> Let us consider how to stir up one another to love and good works, not neglecting to meet together, as is the habit of some, but encouraging one another, and all the more as you see the Day drawing near. (Hebrews 10:24–25)

Although one can pray alone, it is much better to pray together with a congregation. The sages teach that prayer with a congregation is more effective than individuals praying independently.[11] Prayer in a group is nothing magical, nor is it due to any limitation on God's part. Rather, the unity that is achieved as we pray in one accord has merit in and of itself. The merit that arises from togetherness is able to overcome the individual deficits each one of us has.

Jewish law stipulates that there are certain prayers of elevated holiness that may only be prayed in a congregational setting.[12] This is based on Leviticus 22:32, which expresses God's desire to be "sanctified among the people of Israel."

WHAT CONSTITUTES A CONGREGATION?

But what makes a congregation? Two people? Three?

From the perspective of Jewish law, a congregation exists only when a minyan is present. The word *minyan* means "quorum" and consists of a minimum of ten Jewish males at or above the age of bar mitzvah (thirteen). Women, children, and Gentiles are allowed to be part of the congregation, but their presence is not used to determine whether or not a Jewish congregation officially exists.

Liberal forms of Judaism are often uncomfortable with these qualifications because they perceive them as communicating that women are of less value than men. (There is not a significant push in those circles to include children or Gentiles, however.)

The primary and practical reason that women, children, and Gentiles are not counted in a minyan is a matter of obligation. Only those who are obligated to pray at those specific times are counted in the minyan.

Some Modern Orthodox authorities have sanctioned the formation of women-only prayer groups. These are not considered an official minyan, but they do carry out many of the functions of a formal synagogue service.

A similar approach can be taken for Messianic Gentiles. The members of a minyan stand as representatives of an entire community and its households. A minyan of Jews is the baseline definition of a Jewish community. But a community can also be formed of God-fearing Gentiles.

The famous medieval commentator Rabbi Avraham Ibn Ezra addressed a question about Abraham's negotiations with God in Genesis 18: when Abraham pressed for the salvation of Sodom and its neighboring towns, why did he stop at the presence of ten righteous individuals? He dared go so far, but why did he not argue that even one individual was worth sparing the city for?

Rabbi Avraham Ibn Ezra notes,

> Why did he reduce it no further than ten? There are some who say that it was on account of there being two in each city, as there were five cities. But this cannot be correct, since the text says "in Sodom" alone. Even though [we rely on the fact that] our sages of blessed memory decreed that communal prayer cannot be done with less than ten, this source in Scripture bolsters our faith [in the validity their ruling].

In other words, Rabbi Avraham Ibn Ezra sees the potential existence of ten righteous men in Sodom as scriptural evidence for the concept of a minyan for prayer.

Had God found such a minyan in Sodom, it certainly would not have been comprised of Jews. This suggests that there may be validity in considering a community of ten or more men, whether Jewish or not, as a kind of prayer community. This does not necessarily mean that Gentiles should be counted toward a minyan in the traditional sense. However, at the very least, it seems appropriate when ten God-fearing men are present to consider the group to be an official community and able to perform certain community functions.

Nonetheless, we cannot afford to be strict idealists at this stage of Messianic Judaism. In many cases we are laying a foundation for future communities that will one day meet the ideal standards, with God's help. As we are still in the process of creating and building community structures, there may be practical grounds for being lenient in the way we define communities.

GENTILES AND JEWISH PRAYER

It is appropriate for Gentile disciples of Yeshua to participate in Jewish prayer. After all, the Temple in Jerusalem is to be called "a house of prayer for all peoples" (Isaiah 56:7). Yeshua did not come to create a separate religion for Gentiles with different forms of prayer.

Nonetheless, there are issues and boundaries that must be considered when a Gentile chooses to participate in Jewish prayer services. In the same way, the "house of prayer for all peoples" had distinct areas through which men, women, Jews, Gentiles, and priests could enter and different ways in which they participate.

And likewise, just as Gentiles who would visit the Temple courts in Jerusalem would be guests in that Jewish environment, Gentiles who choose to pray Jewish prayers must possess a sense of respect and reverence for the heritage of the Jewish community.

In the ancient Roman Empire, there were Gentiles who aligned with Judaism and participated in the synagogue. They were referred to as God fearers. Cornelius, described in Acts 10, is an example of such a person. The text implies that Cornelius prayed in what seemed to be a Jewish way.

There is a delicate balance when it comes to the relationship of Gentiles to Jewish prayer. If the prayer of Messianic Gentiles is to be identical to Jewish prayer, it implies that these Gentiles have become Jews or that they fit into the same legal category as Jews. This is a type of replacement theology. On the other hand, if

Messianic Gentile prayer is to be completely different from Jewish prayer, it denies the concept that it is through Israel that all nations connect with God.

BLESSINGS IN VAIN

One major component of Jewish prayer is the concept of a blessing. A blessing is not just a nice thing to say about God—it is a careful legal formula invoked at proper occasions.

There is a growing desire among Gentiles to respect and observe Jewish law, or *halachah*. In general that is a good thing. While most *halachah* is directed toward Jews, there is a place in *halachah* for Gentiles as well. *Halachah* does not require everyone to be in the category of "Jews."

One of the main *halachic* concerns with Gentiles praying Jewish prayers is the idea of pronouncing a blessing in vain. This can be a problem whether or not the blessing is made formally. A blessing in vain is a blessing that invokes the name of God but either is recited at an inappropriate time or is a false statement.

For example, if a person recited the proper blessing before eating but had no intention of actually eating, he has recited a blessing in vain. Because he invoked the name of God in an improper way, Jewish law considers it to be a desecration of God's name.

Blessings in vain can also be a false statement. For example, one of the blessings in the Siddur reads, "Blessed are you, O LORD … who has not made me a Gentile." If a person who is not Jewish were to recite this, he would invoke the name of God in connection with a falsehood.

There are also blessings connected with the observance of certain commandments. For example, before wearing tefillin, a Jewish man is to recite, "Blessed are you, O LORD … who has commanded us to lay tefillin." It is inappropriate for a person who is not specifically obligated in that observance to recite the blessing.

Gentiles who are praying Jewish prayers should be careful to avoid prayers like these.

MISAPPROPRIATION OF IDENTITY

The Siddur is written from a first-person Jewish perspective. Naturally, the prayers in it often affirm one's Jewish identity and the special prerogatives of that identity. A Gentile who repeats these statements to himself may begin to see himself as having that identity.

This matters in a congregational setting as well. When a Jew hears a Gentile say, "You chose us and sanctified us out of all the peoples, and you granted your Shabbat as an inheritance to us with love and favor," it can be offensive to him. It can seem like a guest in your home treating your belongings, your wife, and your children as his own.

SOLUTIONS

When arriving at a prayer that results in one of these difficulties, there are a few options as to how a Gentile can proceed:

- In a congregational setting that includes both Jews and Gentiles, the Jewish people who are present could recite the prayer, and others can simply listen and respond with "amen."
- Messianic Gentiles may choose to omit prayers that are inapplicable or have sensitive wording.
- Messianic Gentiles may recite a modified version of the prayer.
- Messianic Gentiles may be creative and intentional in the way they interpret the traditional wording of prayers.

Regarding the third suggestion to modify the prayers, there are two ways that this can be done. One way is to change the first-person wording of the prayer to third person. For example, in a prayer that uses the term "us" to refer to the Jewish people, a Gentile speaker could substitute "your people Israel."

A second way would be to modify the prayer in a way that affirms the specific identity of the Messianic Gentile reader. However, this requires very careful consideration. When making such a change, there could be a temptation to mistakenly imply that Messianic Gentiles benefit spiritually and receive "new covenant" promises, whereas Jews only receive physical or "old covenant" promises.

For example, one line in the traditional after-meal blessing offers thanks to God "for the covenant that [he] sealed in our flesh." It seems problematic for a Messianic Gentile to say this. But should someone who is not Jewish then say "for the covenant that you have written on our hearts"? To do so would imply that Messianic Jews have only a fleshly covenant, whereas the new covenant that is written on hearts belongs only to Messianic Gentiles, God forbid.

Along these lines, substantial portions of synagogue liturgy can still be found in church literature from centuries after the separation of Judaism from Christianity. Often these prayers appear in a modified, more universal form.

However, prayers in a Messianic congregation should not be homogenized. That is, they should not be modified in such a way that both Jews and Gentiles pray the same thing without specifically affirming the identity of either. To do so would be to de-Judaize the prayer and rob Jewish people of the opportunity to express their identity. Rather, Messianic congregations should allow Jews to pray the prayers as they are traditionally written.

The fourth solution for Gentiles praying Jewish prayers—using a creative interpretation of the prayers—is applicable in certain cases. This solution simply means that the Gentile reader should be mindful and aware during prayer and look for ways to think about the prayer or interpret the wording of the prayer so as not to claim Jewish identity. To aid with this, one might begin his prayer with an acknowledgement of his identity as a Messianic Gentile, such as is offered in Part 3 of this book.

WOMEN AND JEWISH PRAYER

According to Jewish law, women too are obligated to pray.[13] Prayer is an essential part of the life of a Jewish woman. In fact, many of the traditions of prayer are derived from the story of Hannah in the Tabernacle at Shiloh (1 Samuel 1–2).

But traditional Judaism recognizes that the form that prayer takes on for women need not be the same as that of men. Jewish tradition places an emphasis for women on spontaneous prayer, the recitation of psalms, and brief supplications.

When possible, women should make a special effort to recite the morning and afternoon prayers, whether individually or with others, especially the most essential parts. However, Jewish law acknowledges that women, especially the mothers of infants and small children, may have time-sensitive priorities that may need to take precedence over scheduled daily prayers. Women also benefit greatly from attending the synagogue, but prayer with a minyan is not a requirement for Jewish women.

YESHUA'S TEACHINGS ABOUT PRAYER

O ur Master Yeshua taught us many important things about prayer. Here is a summary of some of the things he said.

BE PERSISTENT AND INTENSE IN PRAYER

In Luke 18:1–8 Yeshua relates a story about a woman who demanded justice from an unjust judge. Even though the judge did not have any true concern for the woman's case, he granted her request because of her persistence. How much more so will our loving Father in heaven answer our requests if we are persistent with him! The narrator tells us that Yeshua told this parable so that people would pray continually without growing weary (Luke 18:1). Persistence and steadfastness in prayer also appears elsewhere in the New Testament (1 Thessalonians 5:17; Colossians 4:2; Romans 12:12, Ephesians 6:18).

At times Yeshua prayed with fervent intensity. The author of Hebrews wrote, "In the days of his flesh, Jesus offered up prayers and supplications, with loud cries and tears, to him who was able to save him from death, and he was heard because of his reverence" (Hebrews 5:7). Luke described the intensity of his prayer on the night he was betrayed: "Being in an agony he prayed more earnestly; and his sweat became like great drops of blood falling down to the ground" (Luke 22:44).

Pray with Humility

In Luke 18:10–14 Yeshua relates a second story about two men who went to the Temple to pray. One was a Pharisee; the other was a tax collector. The Pharisee boasted in his spirituality; the tax collector acknowledged his sin and begged for mercy.

It is important to note that this parable was not formulated to condemn people for being Pharisees. Rather, the Pharisee was specifically chosen because he represents the "good guy." The Pharisee was someone whom people would have perceived as spiritual, God-fearing, and obedient. The tax collector was a "bad guy" whom people would have perceived as secular, worldly, and ill-intentioned.

In this case we learn that God is not impressed when we boast in our spiritual achievements. The "righteous" one in this case is the one who humbly turned to God in repentance.

Yeshua stressed that we are not to be ceremonious and pray in order to be seen by others. Instead, we should go to a private place, just as our Father himself is unseen (Matthew 6:5–6).

However, Yeshua did also pray in public. He spoke about "when [we] *stand* praying." "Standing" is associated with praying with a congregation, especially at the Temple, where sitting was forbidden. Speaking in front of a crowd, Yeshua said,

> I thank you, Father, Lord of heaven and earth, that you have hidden these things from the wise and understanding and revealed them to little children; yes, Father, for such was your gracious will. (Matthew 11:25–26)

Before raising Lazarus, he prayed publicly:

> Father, I thank you that you have heard me. I knew that you always hear me, but I said this on account of the people standing around, that they may believe that you sent me. (John 11:41–42)

Yeshua did not extend his prayers with needless words. Rather, he taught, "When you pray, do not heap up empty phrases as the Gentiles do, for they think that they will be heard for their many words. Do not be like them, for your Father knows what you need before you ask him" (Matthew 6:7–8).

On the other hand, occasionally he spent extended time in prayer. Mark described how Yeshua arose while it was still dark to pray in a desolate place (Mark 1:35). Before choosing the twelve disciples, he prayed all night long (Luke 6:12–13).

Forgive Others before Turning to God

Yeshua considered forgiveness and reconciliation a prerequisite to prayer. He stated that if we do not forgive others, our Father will not forgive us, as forgiveness from God comes in the merit of forgiveness of others (Matthew 6:12, 14–15; Mark 11:25).

Yeshua went so far as to say that if one is standing in the Temple with a sacrifice in hand and remembers that his brother has something against him, he should leave the sacrifice there and seek reconciliation before offering the sacrifice (Matthew 5:23–24). If this applies when someone has physically made a pilgrimage and is literally standing in the Holy Temple courts in Jerusalem with a sacrifice in hand, how much more would it apply to the much simpler circumstance of prayer at home or in a synagogue!

Have Confidence and Faith

We are to trust that God is all powerful and capable of meeting our needs as well as benevolent and caring. Yeshua's favorite address for God in prayer was "Father." This name for God emphasizes God's compassion toward us and the standing that we have before him as children. Our Master instructed us that when we pray, we are to have faith that we have received our answer (Mark 11:24). If we are faithful, we will receive what we ask for (Matthew 21:22).

Of course, this presumes that we have nullified our own will before God. Even Yeshua himself prayed, "Not my will, but yours, be done" (Luke 22:42).

Our prayers do not have to be fancy, and we do not need to fear that we are not saying the right words or enough of them, since God knows what we need even before we ask (Matthew 6:8). As it is written, "Before they call I will answer; while they are yet speaking I will hear" (Isaiah 65:24).

Pray for Your Enemies

Yeshua taught us to pray for our enemies (Luke 6:28). In context, when Yeshua spoke of enemies, he was not speaking about violent attackers. Rather, enemies are people who are a part of our daily life: people who insult us, take advantage of us, make life difficult for us, or simply rub us the wrong way. They are the people whom we try to avoid or who we refuse to speak to.

We are to pray for these people and show love to them. There is no particular merit in loving and praying for one's friends. That comes naturally. True merit comes from rising above our natural reactions and praying for those who try to hurt us (Matthew 5:44–48).

PART 2

COMMENTARY
ON THE PRAYERS

I Hereby Join

I hereby join myself to the Master, Yeshua the Messiah,
the righteous one, who is the bread of life and the true light,
the source of eternal salvation for all those who hear him.

Like a branch that remains in a vine, so may I remain in
him, just as he also remains in the Father and the Father
in him, in order that they may remain in us.

May the grace of the Master, Yeshua the Messiah, the love
of God, and the fellowship of the Holy Spirit abound to us.

This dedicatory prayer was composed by the staff at First Fruits of Zion. Although apostolic passages form most of its content, it is inspired by Chasidic prayers in which petitioners declare their attachment to a tzaddik (an exceptionally righteous person) before engaging in prayer and observances. For example, a prayer in Breslov tradition expresses the intent to join oneself with Rebbe Nachman. This type of prayer is intended to forge a connection between a disciple and his master (rebbe), even after the tzaddik has passed away.

I Hereby Join

Modern-day Chasidic thought bears remarkable similarity to the ancient writings of the apostles concerning the concept of clinging to the tzaddik. The idea of attaching oneself to a tzaddik arises from a perceived paradox in the Torah. On one hand, the Torah commands us to cling (*davak*, דבק) to God (Deuteronomy 10:20). However, this is problematic since the Torah depicts God as "a consuming fire" (Deuteronomy 4:24). The Chasidic perspective resolves this conflict by employing the tzaddik in the capacity of an intercessor. By attaching oneself to a truly righteous person, one is able to achieve the same level of closeness with God. Chasidic tradition uses this type of prayer to declare and focus on that connection (*hitkashrut*, הִתְקַשְּׁרוּת) before embarking on a time of prayer.

We disciples of Yeshua seek to identify with and attach ourselves to our Master Yeshua, whose righteousness and unity with God is unsurpassed and who intercedes on our behalf before the Father (Hebrews 7:25). In the Master we have an advocate with the Father, "Yeshua the Messiah the tzaddik" (1 John 2:1, author's paraphrase). This Messianic prayer of connection helps disciples of Rabbi Yeshua to focus on the intercession that he performs for us as we pray and on how he is the way to the Father (John 14:6).

"I Hereby Join" draws upon key texts from the New Testament that speak about the *devekut* ("attachment," דְּבֵקוּת) that we have with the Master as he draws and connects us to HaShem. For example, "I in them and you in me, that they may become perfectly one, so that the world may know that you sent me and loved them even as you loved me" (John 17:23). The Messiah is depicted as "the bread of life" (John 6:48) who nourishes our souls with heavenly manna. The imagery of the vine in this prayer aptly symbolizes our critical bond with the Master: "Abide in me, and I in you. As the branch cannot bear fruit by itself, unless it abides in the vine, neither can you, unless you abide in me" (John 15:4). This tapestry of passages speaks of the beautiful and awe-inspiring union that we attain with HaShem by our identity in Messiah Yeshua.

DECLARATION OF INTENT FOR MESSIANIC GENTILES

G entiles who devote themselves to Yeshua of Nazareth are not only disciples; they are his subjects, and he is their King. In that sense they relate to the nation of Israel and the Jewish people in the same way that a conquered and annexed people is subordinated to a conquering king. These Gentiles are no longer separated from the Messiah or "alienated from the commonwealth of Israel and strangers to the covenants of promise" (Ephesians 2:12). Instead, they share in the inheritance and the destiny of the whole nation. In keeping with this identity, the God-fearing Messianic Gentile should not hesitate to join the Jewish people in formal prayer.

At the same time, there are also Jewish disciples of Yeshua; their Jewishness remains significant, and it is central to their unique identity. Unity in corporate prayer between Messianic Gentiles and Jews is a beautiful and powerful testimony of Yeshua's greatness. Such unity can only exist in a setting in which members are aware of their respective roles within the people of God.

Jewish people composed the prayer service in a way that reflected their identity as Jews. As Messianic Gentiles engage in these prayers, they must not lose sight of their own important and esteemed position as the crowning jewels of the nations. A Messianic Gentile who participates in the prayers and petitions of Israel should thus consciously acknowledge that since he is not legally Jewish, his connection to Israel comes only through King Messiah. To facilitate this awareness, we recommend that Messianic Gentiles undertake a brief meditation and declaration of intent prior to participating in formal Jewish prayer.

The declaration of intent printed in Part 3 of this book was composed by the staff of First Fruits of Zion and inspired by the prayers of the Gentile Sabbatarian community that once thrived in Transylvania.

OPENING WORDS

> *With the permission of the heavenly assembly, and with the permission of the earthly assembly, I hereby prepare my mouth to thank, praise, laud, petition, and serve my creator in the words of his people Israel.*

The opening words of the meditation borrow language from similar declarations of intention that appear in many Siddurim for using prior to undertaking a mitzvah or a particular order of prayer.

GENTILE BRANCHES

The next passage is based on a similar disclaimer that the Gentile Sabbatarians of Transylvania composed for their own prayer books:

> *I cannot declare that Abraham fathered me, nor can I claim to be his offspring according to the flesh. For I am a branch from the stem of the children of Shem, Ham, and Japheth.*

As do Messianic Gentiles today, the Transylvanian Sabbatarians employed prayers and liturgical traditions derived from Judaism. Paul teaches that Gentile believers should regard themselves as the spiritual sons and daughters of Abraham but not in the same physical and legal sense that Jews do:

> *Like a wild olive branch grafted into a cultivated olive tree, in order to sprout forth and produce fruit in the name of all Israel …*

In Romans 11, Paul compares the Gentile believer to a branch cut from a wild olive tree (another nation) and grafted into the olive tree of Israel: "You, although a wild olive shoot, were grafted in among the others and now share in the nourishing root of the olive tree" (Romans 11:17).

SONS AND DAUGHTERS OF GOD THROUGH MESSIAH

The old Sabbatarian prayers from Transylvania declare that since the Gentile believer cannot boast in his legal status as a Jew or as a literal descendant of Father Abraham, he rejoices in the heavenly Father alone:

> *Father, who is in heaven, I will rejoice in you alone.*

In a similar way, Paul declared that even Jewish believers should "put no confidence in the flesh" (Philippians 3:3–4), even though he had reason to do so. Rather, both Jews and Gentiles should rely upon and rejoice in their Father in heaven.

The prayer continues,

> *You have made me a son of Abraham through your King Messiah.*

In this context the term "son of Abraham" implies both sons and daughters. The Gentile believer in Yeshua adopts the faith of Abraham and lays hold of the promises that God made to Abraham. In Messiah, Gentile believers are "Abraham's offspring" and "heirs according to promise" (Galatians 3:28–29). Through the Messianic promises, Abraham has become a "father of many nations" (Romans 4:17), "not only to the adherent of the law but also to the one who shares the faith of Abraham, who is the father of us all" (Romans 4:16).

IN THE NAME OF YESHUA

Believers pray in the name of Yeshua (John 14:13–14, 15:16, 16:23–24), meaning that we invoke the merit and virtue of our holy Master and approach God as Yeshua's agents. In a similar way, the Gentile believer joins his prayers with those of the whole nation of Israel:

For the sake of our Master Yeshua, in his merit and virtues, may the sayings of my mouth and meditation of my heart be joined to the prayers of all Israel, and may they be favorable before you, O LORD, my rock and my redeemer.

The Shma

The *Shma* is a collection of passages from Scripture that observant Jews recite at least twice each day as a part of the daily prayers. This recitation is likely the oldest component of the daily prayer ritual. The text itself dates back to Moses.

The reading is composed of three parts. The first part comes from Deuteronomy 6:4–9. It declares the oneness of God and states the command to love him. It continues by describing how Israel must fixate on God's words and recite them continually.

Jewish tradition holds that the instructions to "fasten them to your hand as a sign, and let them be ornaments between your eyes" (Deuteronomy 6:8, author's translation) allude to the commandment to wear tefillin. These are boxes made of leather that contain scrolls on which short passages of Scripture are written. Observant Jewish men literally bind them to the arm and head with leather straps during prayer and study.

The instructions "write them upon the doorposts of your home and on your gates" (Deuteronomy 6:9, author's translation) are similarly interpreted to refer to the mezuzah. A mezuzah is a small case in which a scroll is inserted. Observant Jews affix these cases at about eye level alongside the doors of the home.

The second reading from which the *Shma* comes is Deuteronomy 11:13–21. This passage focuses on the blessings for obedience and the consequences of disregarding God's laws. It employs the same language that is interpreted as referring to the tefillin and the mezuzah.

The third reading from which the *Shma* is taken is different from the other two. It comes from Numbers 15:37–41, which speaks of the commandment to wear a tassel called a tzitzit on each of the four corners of a garment. The passage continues by invoking the exodus from Egypt.

In a complete prayer service, the *Shma* is surrounded by blessings. Two blessings are recited beforehand, and one is recited afterward. The content of these blessings is different in the morning prayers than it is in the evening prayers, but the blessings contain similar ideas. The first blessing, whether morning or evening, relates to God as the creator of all, in particular of the luminaries of heaven and of the passage of time. The second blessing focuses on the special covenant of love that God shares with Israel as expressed in the Torah. The third blessing, which comes after the three paragraphs of the *Shma*, acknowledges God as Redeemer.

The blessings before and after the *Shma* are some of the oldest extra-biblical prayers in the Siddur, dating back in some form to the time of the apostles. The combination of scriptural passages that comprise the paragraphs of the *Shma* is attested in ancient tefillin that archaeologists have found.

The Significance of the Shma

The *Shma* means much more to Judaism than simply a Scripture reading or a daily prayer. It is a summary of faith, mission, and identity all in one. The verses in it are often the first from the Bible that a Jewish child learns by heart. It is recited at least twice daily by faithful Jewish people for as long as they live. Many people, especially martyrs, utter the words of the *Shma* with their dying breath.

Yeshua affirmed the central nature of this passage. Mark 12:28–30 records the conversation in which he did so:

> One of the scribes came up and heard them disputing with one another, and seeing that he answered them well, asked him, "Which commandment is the most important of all?" Jesus answered, "The most important is, 'Hear, O Israel: The LORD our God, the LORD is one. And you shall love the LORD your God with all your heart and with all your soul and with all your mind and with all your strength."

HEAR, O ISRAEL: THE YOKE OF THE KINGDOM

Hear, O Israel! The LORD is our God; the LORD is one.

Reciting the first line of the *Shma* is referred to by the sages as "accepting the yoke of the kingdom of heaven." It is a way of saying, "God is my King. I will serve him and no other." (In rabbinic literature "the kingdom of heaven" is not synonymous with the Messianic Era, as it was with Yeshua. It simply referred to God's rulership and authority.)

The *Shma* is recited twice each day: once in the evening and again the next morning. This is based on the phrase "when you lie down, and when you arise." This shows that accepting God's authority and loving instructions is not something one does only once in life. Rather, our resolve to remain loyal to God and to heed him must be renewed every day.

One covers the eyes with the right hand while saying the first line. The earliest mention of covering the eyes when saying the *Shma* is found in the Talmud. It describes how Rabbi Judah, the compiler of the Mishnah, would briefly interrupt his morning study in order to say the *Shma* at the proper time. As he did so, he would pass his hand over his eyes.

The *Shma* is a foundational and important component of the prayer service. During the first line of the *Shma*, one should make extra effort to focus on its meaning. Covering the eyes is done in order to achieve maximum concentration and to avoid distraction.

BLESSED IS THE NAME

Blessed is the name of the glory
of his kingdom forever and ever.

After the first line of the *Shma*, we insert the declaration, "Blessed is the name of the glory of his kingdom forever and ever." This dates back to Temple practice. When the name of God was pronounced aloud in the Temple, all the people immediately prostrated themselves and proclaimed this line aloud. This insertion is based on Psalm 72:19: "Blessed be his glorious name forever; may the whole earth be filled with his glory! Amen and Amen!"

In the daily prayers, "Blessed is the name," is recited in a whisper, except on Yom Kippur, when it is declared aloud. This symbolizes the fact that although God is King, his kingship is not fully revealed in the world today. People go about their daily lives without even noticing or acknowledging God's presence and reign. Yom Kippur represents the future time in the Messianic Era when "every knee will bow" and all will acknowledge God as King.

A third century rabbi named Shimon ben Lakish explained why this line was added to the *Shma* with a midrashic story.[14] The Torah describes in Genesis 49 how Jacob gathered his children together to reveal what would happen in the "last days." According to the explanation of Rabbi Shimon, Jacob hesitated out of concern that one of them might be flawed like Ishmael or Esau. When his sons saw his concern, they all expressed their faithfulness to God by saying the *Shma* in unison. "Hear, O Israel," they said (after all, Israel was Jacob's name), "the LORD is our God; the LORD is one."

When Jacob heard how committed they were to serving God, he joyfully responded, "Blessed is the name of the glory of his kingdom forever and ever!" The rabbis reasoned that if Jacob said this in response to the *Shma*, so should we. On the other hand, they also reasoned, since Moses did not include it in the text of the Torah, so we shouldn't either. The sages decided that as a compromise, we should say it but quietly.

The midrash provides another tradition about where this line comes from. According to this story, Moses heard the angels saying "Blessed is the name" while he stood in the heavenly realm atop Mount Sinai. It was a secret part of the angelic worship service. The reason we say these words so quietly is because they are a special treasure not intended for humans. Moses was like a man who stole jewelry from the king's palace and gave it to his wife. He made sure to tell her, "Don't wear these in public!" But on Yom Kippur, when people are like the angels in purity and God's kingship is openly revealed, this line is recited out loud.

Neither of these stories is meant to be taken literally or historically. They simply help us to understand the significance of the words.

FIRST PARAGRAPH:
LOVE THE LORD YOUR GOD

> *Love the LORD, your God, with all your heart, with all your*
> *soul, and with all your might. Let these words that I com-*
> *mand you today be on your heart. Teach them repeatedly*
> *to your children, and speak of them when you sit in your*
> *home, when you walk on the road, when you lie down,*
> *and when you arise. Fasten them to your hand as a sign,*
> *and let them be ornaments between your eyes. Write them*
> *upon the doorposts of your home and on your gates.*

Yeshua, in Matthew 22:36–37, identified the commandment to love God as the greatest commandment in the Torah. In Mark 12:28–30 it is called the most important (literally "first"). In Luke 10:28 Yeshua remarks regarding this commandment, "Do this, and you will live."

Yeshua taught that the second commandment is found in Leviticus 19:18: "Love your neighbor as yourself." In connecting these two verses, Yeshua employed a rabbinic principle of Torah interpretation called *gezerah shavah* (גְּזֵרָה שָׁוָה). In this hermeneutical method, passages in the Scriptures are compared to one another based on similar wording. In this case both verses begin with the Hebrew word *ve'ahavta* ("You shall love," וְאָהַבְתָּ).

Gezerah shavah is typically used to prove the similarity or equivalence of different passages. In this case Yeshua's point was not simply to say that loving God is of utmost importance and that loving one's fellow ranks second. It was common knowledge that loving God was of prime importance. Rather, Yeshua was making the argument that loving one's fellow is so important that it is equivalent to love of God.

When reciting the commandment to love God, one should concentrate on accepting and fulfilling this command. Considering our Master's teaching, one should also have in mind that loving God implies loving others, since the two commandments are fundamentally the same.

It is essential that we accept the yoke of these two commandments first, because "on these two commandments depend all the Law and the Prophets" (Matthew 22:40).

The concept of love of God flows naturally from the realization that God is one. Since God is one and there are no other gods,
everything in creation ultimately comes from him. "From him and
through him and to him are all things" (Romans 11:36). All that we
have and are belongs to him, so it is fitting for us to submit ourselves
to him with our whole being.

It seems that love should be a feeling that flows naturally and
organically. How can we be *commanded* to love someone? Rashi
explained that this mandate to love the LORD our God means that
when we obey God's commands, we should seek to do so out of
love rather than out of fear. One who obeys out of fear does not
want to be subservient; he already has one foot out the door. But
one who serves out of love is like a servant who says, "I love my
master." When he is freed during the Jubilee Year, he chooses to
stay and continue serving his master (Exodus 21:5–6).

We are commanded to love with all our "heart," "soul," and
"might." These terms are significant; using them is not simply a
poetic way of saying "very much."

HEART

Although in Western culture we tend to think of the heart as the
seat of our emotions, in biblical symbolism the heart refers to the
will and the mind.

A human being has two inclinations—two forces that motivate
us—that can be seen as components of the heart. In Judaism today
they are referred to as the *yetzer ha-tov* ("the good inclination,"
יֵצֶר הַטּוֹב) and the *yetzer ha-ra* ("the evil inclination," יֵצֶר הָרַע). The
New Testament sometimes employs "spirit" and "flesh" to convey
similar ideas.

The good inclination is what drives us to be more spiritual
and to connect closely to God. It presses us toward selflessness
and altruism.

"Flesh" is actually a more appropriate term than "evil inclination," since this force within us is not inherently evil. Rather, this
term represents our animalistic side. It is the part of humanity that
we share with animals; it supplies us with a desire to preserve our
lives; to be gratified with pleasure; and to eat, sleep, reproduce,
and protect ourselves from harm. Unchecked, the flesh can lead

to selfishness and wickedness. But just as a horse that is tamed, harnessed, and controlled by a wagon driver serves to increase the driver's capacity for transportation, when the flesh is subjugated by the spirit, it has the capacity to multiply one's efforts to serve God.

To love God with the whole heart is to serve him with both our physical and spiritual desires. This also means loving him with a heart that is undivided by uncertainty or double-mindedness.

SOUL

The Hebrew word translated "soul" is *nefesh* (נֶפֶשׁ). *Nefesh* refers to a person's life, self, or life force. The *nefesh* is what animates a person, and it departs when one dies. To love God with one's soul is to place one's devotion to God at a higher priority than one's own life. Yeshua exhibited this type of love when he laid down his life, saying, "Not my will, but yours, be done" (Luke 22:42).

In Judaism having a sincere intention to do something is considered equal in the eyes of God to actually performing the deed. Thus, if we sincerely express our true willingness to sacrifice our lives as martyrs for God, it is reckoned as if we have actually given our lives. Even in the absence of an actual threat, we commit to loving God with our soul—that is, being willing to suffer death for the sake of God—each day in the recital of the *Shma*. The commentary *Bayit Chadash* states that this is the meaning of Psalm 44:23[22]: "For your sake we are killed all the day long; we are regarded as sheep to be slaughtered."

Paul quotes this verse in Romans 8:36, instructing the reader to be confident in the face of persecution and danger, since these will not separate him from the love of the Messiah.

Yeshua spoke about being willing to give up one's life for the kingdom. He instructed,

> If anyone would come after me, let him deny himself and take up his cross and follow me. For whoever would save his life will lose it, but whoever loses his life for my sake and the gospel's will save it. For what does it profit a man to gain the whole world and forfeit his soul? For what can a man give in return for his soul? (Mark 8:34–37)

When Rabbi Akiva was taken to be tortured to death by the Romans, it was the time of the recital of the morning *Shma*. He told his students, "All my life I have been troubled by the phrase 'with all your soul,' which means 'even if he takes your soul.' I thought, 'When will I be able to fulfill this commandment?'" While they tore away his flesh with iron combs, he recited the *Shma* with his dying breath.[15]

MIGHT

The Hebrew word translated "might" does not refer to literal strength. The Hebrew word is *me'od* (מְאֹד), which is normally an adverb that intensifies an adjective or verb, as do the English words "very" or "greatly." But in this passage it is strangely treated as a noun, resulting in an awkward phrase that sounds like "with all your greatly."

Rashi interprets this difficult phrase to mean "with all of your *mamon* [wealth]." That is to say, we are to love God with all our material strength, our physical resources at hand, and particularly our money. This interpretation is also reflected in the Targums, the ancient Aramaic translations of the Hebrew Scriptures.

This understanding is in keeping with our Master Yeshua's teaching. Yeshua commended the poor widow for donating her entire livelihood to the Temple treasury (Mark 12:41–44; Luke 21:1–4). She truly loved God with all her *me'od*. Yeshua told the rich young ruler, "Sell all you have and give it to the poor" (Matthew 19:21; Mark 10:21; Luke 18:22). He warned others that they cannot serve both God and *mamon* (Matthew 6:24; Luke 16:13).

The love of God in turn progresses naturally to our learning, teaching, and meditating on his words, as described in the continuing paragraph of the recitation (Deuteronomy 6:6–9).

WITH ALL YOUR "MIND"?

When Yeshua quoted Deuteronomy 6:5 from the Torah, did he deviate from the original wording? The Torah uses three Hebrew terms to describe with what we must love God. The Septuagint also uses three Greek terms:

Torah	Septuagint	Septuagint Translation
levav (לְבָב)	*kardia* (καρδία)	heart
nefesh (נֶפֶשׁ)	*psuche* (ψυχή)	soul
me'od (מְאֹד)	*dunamis* (δύναμις)	power

But when this passage is quoted in the Gospels, it seems to be recorded differently. The Gospel of Matthew quotes Yeshua using the Greek term *dianoia* (διάνοια) in the place of *me'od*. *Dianoia* is typically translated "mind."

One might think that this word choice reflects a unique and new interpretation given by Yeshua. However, the same wording appears in Luke, where a "lawyer" quotes the verse using the term *dianoia* in just the same way.

Further complicating matters, the Gospel of Mark records Yeshua's teaching on this verse with a fourth Greek term: *ischus* (ἰσχύς). *Ischus* means "strength," which is fairly similar to the Septuagint's *dunamis* ("power").

This leaves us with a few questions. Why do the Gospels employ the term *dianoia* ("mind"), when the Torah does not seem to say anything about the mind? Why does Mark's version contain four terms instead of three? What did Yeshua actually say when he quoted this verse?

Yeshua would not have quoted the verse in Greek at all. The authors of the Gospels faithfully transmitted his teachings to us using the Greek language, but they were recording conversations that would have taken place in Hebrew or Aramaic. It seems particularly likely, with such a famous and central verse such as this, that Yeshua would have quoted it in Hebrew directly from the Torah.

That means that the decision to use *dianoia*, and in Mark's case, to use four terms instead of three, reflects the stylistic decisions of those who interpreted Yeshua's teachings into Greek. They do not directly rest upon Yeshua's teaching itself. In the case of Mark, the author must have felt that the three terms used in the Torah could not be expressed adequately using only three Greek terms.

But this still leaves the question: why did the writers of the Gospels choose *dianoia* instead of simply using the Septuagint's *dunamis* ("power") or Mark's *ischus* ("strength")?

The Hebrew translation of the Gospels by Franz Delitzsch helps to provide an interesting suggestion. Delitzsch translated the Greek *dianoia* using the Hebrew term *madda* (מַדָּע), which means "knowledge." Could the similarity of *me'od* and *madda* have inspired an interpretation of *me'od* as "mind"? This suggestion is merely speculative, but it would explain the choice of *dianoia* among the writers of the Gospels in Greek.

THE THREE PRIVATE DEEDS: PRAYER, FASTING, AND GIVING

In *Torah Club: Chronicles of the Messiah,* D.T. Lancaster notes the connection between the *Shma* and Yeshua's teaching about private deeds of righteousness.

The *Shma* describes three spheres of love toward God. One is to love him with the heart (*levav*), soul, (*nefesh*), and might (*me'od*). Similarly, in Matthew 6, Yeshua describes three acts of devotion that one must perform in modest privacy: prayer, fasting, and giving.

The sages of the Midrash derived a similar triad from Scripture:

> Three things nullify harsh decrees: prayer (*tefillah*), charity (*tzedakah*), and repentance (*teshuvah*). The three of them are mentioned in one verse (2 Chronicles 7:14):
>
> - "If my people who are called by my name humble themselves, and pray"—this is prayer.
>
> - "And seek my face"—this is charity [*tzedakah*], as it is written, "I shall behold your face in righteousness [*tzedek*]" (Psalm 17:15).
>
> - "And turn from their wicked ways"—this is repentance.
>
> Afterwards it says, "Then I will hear from heaven and will forgive their sin and heal their land."[16]

Prayer

Prayer corresponds to the act of loving God with one's heart. The priests' sacrificial duties in the Temple constitute "service," which in Hebrew is *avodah*. But we are all commanded to serve God with our heart (Deuteronomy 10:12). The sages identify the service of the heart (*avodah shebalev*) as prayer. Yeshua taught that the words on one's lips issue forth from one's heart: "Out of the abundance of the heart the mouth speaks" (Matthew 12:34). At the conclusion of praying the *Amidah*, it is traditional to recite Psalm 19:15[14]: "Let the words of my mouth and the meditation of my heart be acceptable in your sight, O LORD, my rock and my redeemer."

Yeshua taught that we must pray discreetly: "When you pray, go into your room and shut the door and pray to your Father who is in secret. And your Father who sees in secret will reward you" (Matthew 6:6).

Fasting

Fasting corresponds to the act of loving God with one's soul, and it is closely linked to repentance. The Hebrew word translated "soul" is *nefesh*. In Biblical Hebrew this refers to a human's life and vitality. The Bible speaks of fasting as afflicting one's soul. For example, Psalm 35:13 says, "I afflicted myself [literally "my *nefesh*"] with fasting." Isaiah 58:3 expresses in a couplet of Biblical Hebrew poetry, "Why have we fasted, and you see it not? Why have we humbled ourselves [literally "afflicted our *nefesh*"], and you take no knowledge of it?"

One purpose of fasting is to facilitate repentance as one's fleshly desires are set aside to focus on God's will. It also serves as a type of divine worship. Rav Sheshet, a late third-century rabbi, would offer this prayer on fast days:

> Master of all worlds, you know that when the Temple was still standing, a person who sinned could bring a sacrifice. The only parts that were offered were the fat and blood, and they atoned for him. Now, I have sat fasting, reducing my own fat and blood as though I offered them to you on the altar. Show me favor.[17]

Yeshua taught about fasting with true humility:

> When you fast, do not look gloomy like the hypocrites, for they disfigure their faces that their fasting may be seen by others. Truly, I say to you, they have received their reward. But when you fast, anoint your head and wash your face, that your fasting may not be seen by others but by your Father who is in secret. And your Father who sees in secret will reward you. (Matthew 6:16–18)

Yeshua's admonition does not relate to public obligatory fasts such as Yom Kippur. If a Jewish person were to pretend not to be fasting on that day, it would be tantamount to pretending to sin; it would actually be the appearance of evil! Rather, Yeshua is describing the proper behavior of one who engages in a private, voluntary fast. Notice that by his words "when you fast," our Master takes it for granted that we will at times fast.

GIVING

Giving to charity corresponds to the act of loving God with one's might. Since *me'od* corresponds to *mamon* (wealth), one must express his love for God through giving generously of his money and physical resources.

Yeshua taught about how our giving must be discreet as well:

> When you give to the needy, do not let your left hand know what your right hand is doing, so that your giving may be in secret. And your Father who sees in secret will reward you. (Matthew 6:3–4)

Each of these acts of devotion relate to the commandment to love God. Thus, to a certain degree we may interpret Deuteronomy 6:5 to say, "Love the LORD your God through prayer, through fasting, and through giving."

HEART, SOUL, AND MIGHT IN THE PARABLE OF THE SOWER

The pattern of heart, soul, and might also appear in the parable of the sower:

He told them many things in parables, saying: "A sower went out to sow. And as he sowed, some seeds fell along the path, and the birds came and devoured them. Other seeds fell on rocky ground, where they did not have much soil, and immediately they sprang up, since they had no depth of soil, but when the sun rose they were scorched. And since they had no root, they withered away. Other seeds fell among thorns, and the thorns grew up and choked them. Other seeds fell on good soil and produced grain, some a hundredfold, some sixty, some thirty. He who has ears, let him hear." (Matthew 13:3–9)

Note Yeshua's direction to "hear," which he repeats in his interpretation:

Hear then the parable of the sower: When anyone hears the word of the kingdom and does not understand it, the evil one comes and snatches away what has been sown in his heart. This is what was sown along the path. As for what was sown on rocky ground, this is the one who hears the word and immediately receives it with joy, yet he has no root in himself, but endures for a while, and when tribulation or persecution arises on account of the word, immediately he falls away. As for what was sown among thorns, this is the one who hears the word, but the cares of the world and the deceitfulness of riches choke the word, and it proves unfruitful. As for what was sown on good soil, this is the one who hears the word and understands it. He indeed bears fruit and yields, in one case a hundredfold, in another sixty, and in another thirty. (Matthew 13:18–23)

Each of the elements of the heart, soul, and might are present in this parable. The first three individuals are those who fail in one of the three types of love; the fourth is the one who succeeds in loving God with heart, soul, and might:

- Heart: The first does not *understand*. In Hebraic thought, understanding takes place in the heart.

Thus the evil one snatches away what is in his *heart*.

- Soul: The second fails on account of tribulation and persecution. He is unwilling to give up his soul, that is, his life, on account of the message.
- Might: The third is overtaken by the pursuit of *mamon*, wealth. He fails to love God with the resources that make him mighty.

Thus we can see that in this parable, Yeshua was teaching about the *Shma*. This helps us to understand his interpretation of the command to love God.

ON YOUR HEART

The heart is the seat of the will and mind in biblical symbolism. When the Torah says that its words shall be on our heart, it indicates that our thoughts are to be focused on God's words continually.

One of the new-covenant promises is that the Torah will be written on our hearts (Jeremiah 31:32[33]). This indicates that it will become a part of our nature to follow it.

The *Shma* makes it clear that loving God is not something that can be compartmentalized. We are to obsess over God's words. We are not only to teach them to our children, we are to drill the Torah into our children's minds and identities. Talk about God's commandments is not to be relegated to weekly gatherings, but our faith should be expressed everywhere we go and in every waking hour.

A SIGN AND AN ORNAMENT

The text of the *Shma* states that "these words" are to be bound to the hand and placed as an ornament between the eyes. In Jewish practice this refers to the practice of wearing tefillin. Tefillin are black boxes made of leather. They have compartments that contain scrolls on which are written these covenant-related passages from Scripture. Sometimes they are referred to as phylacteries.

In the era of the disciples, observant Jews wore tefillin all day long, although the boxes were smaller than they are today. Archaeologists have discovered ancient tefillin among other remains, and they bear many similarities to the type worn today.

Yeshua referred to tefillin when he said that certain hypocrites "make their phylacteries broad" (Matthew 23:5). However, he did not criticize the use of tefillin, which was normative Jewish practice at the time, but only the wearing of them in an ostentatious manner. We have every reason to believe that Yeshua and his disciples wore tefillin on a daily basis.

Tefillin are a distinct marker of Jewish identity. It is not forbidden for a Messianic Gentile to wear them; however, there are some communities in which it would be confusing or even offensive for a non-Jew to do so. It is important that Messianic Gentiles who wear tefillin are sensitive to the message that it communicates and that they conform to community standards; it may be advisable for Messianic Gentiles to avoid wearing them in public venues.

Traditionally Judaism teaches that the mitzvah of tefillin applies specifically to Jewish men; women are not obligated to wear them and are discouraged from doing so. In liberal and egalitarian forms of Judaism, some women choose to wear them.

SECOND PARAGRAPH:
If You Dutifully Heed My Commandments

If you dutifully heed my commandments that I command you today, to love the LORD your God and to serve him with all your heart and with all your soul, then I will provide rain for your land in its time: the autumn rain and the spring rain. You will gather in your grain, your fresh wine, and your fine oil. And I will provide grass in your fields for your cattle, and you will eat and be satisfied.

Guard yourselves, or else your hearts will be seduced, and you will stray and serve other gods and bow in worship to them. Then the LORD's anger will flare up against you. He will seal off heaven so there will be no rain, and the ground will not give you its harvest. You will quickly perish from the good land that the LORD is giving you.

*So place these words of mine upon your heart and upon
your soul. Fasten them to your hand as a sign, and let them
be ornaments between your eyes. Teach them to your children, speaking of them when you sit in your home, when
you walk on the road, when you lie down, and when you
arise. Write them upon the doorposts of your home and
on your gates. Do this so that your days and the days of
your children may be abundant upon the ground that the
LORD swore to give to your fathers for as long as heaven
is above the earth.*

Whereas reciting the first line of the *Shma* is called "accepting
the yoke of the kingdom of heaven," reciting the remainder of the
Shma's first paragraph and the paragraph that follows is referred
to as "accepting the yoke of the commandments." By reciting this
passage we declare our acceptance of the rules and instructions
that God has given.

The second portion of the *Shma* takes the progression a step
further than the first. Rather than simply learning or contemplat-
ing the laws of God, this section focuses on the consequences of
either fulfilling or neglecting the commandments. The sages asked,

Why does the passage "Hear, O Israel" come before "If
you dutifully heed"? It is so that one may first accept the
yoke of the kingdom of heaven and then afterward the
yoke of the commandments.[18]

The reward or punishment meted out in this passage relates to
the benefits of rain on the land. The land of Israel receives its rain
as the direct result of God's involvement. Moses explains,

The land that you are going over to possess is a land of
hills and valleys, which drinks water by the rain from
heaven, a land that the LORD your God cares for. The
eyes of the LORD your God are always upon it, from the
beginning of the year to the end of the year. (Deuteronomy 11:11–12)

In reward for obedience, Moses promises that Israel will see an
abundance of crops. This simple promise paints a picture of Israel
in a time of redemption: obedience to Torah, abundant rainfall,

plentiful crops, and satisfaction. These features echo the promises of the new covenant and the depiction of the Messianic Era found in Deuteronomy 30.

The punishment for disobedience is not only a lack of rain; it ultimately leads to exile. Not only does the rain stop, but God "will seal off heaven." This implies not only a lack of rain but a barrier between Israel and God, as if God will remain hidden.

God is just. On a fundamental level justice is carried out when people get what they deserve, whether good or bad. Thus, when the righteous are rewarded or the wicked are punished, justice is performed, and an aspect of godliness is revealed in the world. When the opposite occurs, it is as if God's true nature is obscured.

Rain is a sign that the heavens are opened, and God is revealed in the world. This can be good or bad, depending on which side of justice one falls. At the flood in the days of Noah, "the windows of the heavens were opened" (Genesis 7:11), bringing destruction. When God promised Noah that "never again shall all flesh be cut off by the waters of the flood, and never again shall there be a flood to destroy the earth" (Genesis 9:11), it meant that God would take a new approach to dealing with mankind. Rather than "opening the heavens" to destroy the wicked immediately, God would close off the heavens and distance himself, sparing the wicked for a time in order that they may repent.

In the second paragraph of the *Shma*, we learn that when Israel is righteous, God will conduct himself with justice, reveal himself, and grant reward. When Israel is disobedient, God will obscure himself. Although this is unpleasant and results in Israel's temporary banishment from the land, it is an act of mercy, because it spares Israel from direct judgment.

THIRD PARAGRAPH:
MAKE FOR THEMSELVES A TZITZIT

> *The LORD said to Moses, "Speak to the children of Israel and tell them to make for themselves a tzitzit on each of the corners of their garments throughout their generations. And they are to give the tzitzit of the corner a cord of techelet. It will be a tzitzit for you, and you will see them*

and remember all the LORD's commandments and carry them out.

You must not explore after your heart or after your eyes, which lead you to act unfaithfully. Do this so that you remember and carry out all my commandments, and you will be holy for your God. I am the LORD your God who brought you out from the land of Egypt to be your God. I am the LORD your God."

The third paragraph of the *Shma* was included because it alludes to several important elements of Jewish faith and practice that relate to the pursuit of holiness and sanctification.

WEARING TZITZIYOT

The text of the *Shma* commands, "Tell them to make for themselves a tzitzit on each of the corners of their garments." This ritual brings special distinction to Israel, like a mark of God's special ownership.

Tzitziyot are tassels made from strings that are knotted and tied in a special way and attached to the corners of a garment. The singular form of the word is tzitzit. *Tzitziyot* are attached to a large shawl called a *tallit,* which is worn by Jewish men during morning prayer and study. They can also be found on a small four-cornered undergarment called a *tallit katan,* which is usually worn under a shirt or vest by Jewish males throughout the day.

Numbers 15:38 mentions that each tzitzit is to include a cord of *techelet. Techelet* is a type of blue dye that comes from a sea creature (perhaps a snail) found in the Mediterranean Sea. Over the centuries the identity of this creature was lost. Today there are multiple opinions as to the correct source of this dye. Since the identity of the proper source of *techelet* is uncertain, most observant Jews wear only white *tzitziyot*. However, wearing *tzitziyot* with *techelet* is gaining in popularity, especially in Israel.

Decades ago, some people involved in Jewish evangelism adopted the practice of attaching tzitzit-like fringes to the belt loops on their trousers. This was intended to give the illusion that they were wearing *tzitziyot* in the manner of an observant Jew, since the fringes were roughly located in the same place as one would wear a *tallit katan*.

Unfortunately, this practice caught on quickly among people involved in Hebrew Roots and Messianic Judaism. Many people are unaware that this is not the normal way to wear *tzitziyot*. Wearing tassels on the belt loops does not fulfill the biblical commandment in Deuteronomy 22:12, which indicates that the tassels are to be attached to a four-cornered garment called a *kesut* (כְּסוּת). The term *kesut* refers to a cloak-like garment that covers the shoulders. Furthermore, to people who are familiar with the proper custom, *tzitziyot* worn on belt loops look like an outlandish impersonation of actual Jewish practice.

When wearing a *tallit katan*, the *tzitziyot* do not need to be exposed; many Jews from both Ashkenazi and Sephardi communities keep them hidden.

Tzitziyot serve as a marker of Jewish identity. It is not forbidden for Messianic Gentiles to wear them; however, doing so may cause confusion and offense. It is advisable for Messianic Gentiles who choose to wear them to do so with utter discretion.

Traditional Judaism considers women to be exempt from wearing *tzitziyot*, and historically it has been very uncommon for women to wear them. In liberal and egalitarian forms of Judaism, it is more common for women to choose to wear them.

All disciples should bear in mind the Master's instructions about modesty in such matters (Matthew 23:11–12).

THE YOKE OF THE COMMANDMENTS

The purpose of the *tzitziyot* is that the wearer "will see them and remember all the LORD's commandments and carry them out." The commandments themselves sanctify Israel, since by observing them the people lead holy lives, which sets them apart from the other nations. As Peter wrote, "As he who called you is holy, you also be holy in all your conduct, since it is written, 'You shall be holy, for I am holy'" (1 Peter 1:15–16).

THE EXODUS FROM EGYPT

The text of the prayer says, "God … brought you out from the land of Egypt to be your God." By reciting this line with intention, one fulfills the commandment to remember the exodus from Egypt every day (Deuteronomy 16:3).

PROPER BELIEF IN GOD

Although beliefs and doctrines are not strongly emphasized in Judaism, there are certain fundamental ideas that one must hold as a bare minimum. One is the belief that God exists.

But where is this concept found in this passage of the *Shma*? The sages connect it midrashically. The prayer says, "You must not explore after your *heart*" (emphasis added). Likewise, we read in Psalm 14:1, "The fool says in his *heart*, 'There is no God'" (emphasis added). Thus, "exploring after one's heart" refers to lacking belief in God. The author of Hebrews explains, "Without faith it is impossible to please him, for whoever would draw near to God must believe that he exists and that he rewards those who seek him" (Hebrews 11:6).

SEXUAL PURITY

The text of the prayer tells us, "You must not explore … after your eyes." The sages saw this as a reference to sexual immorality, based on Judges 14:3: "Samson said to his father, 'Get her for me, for she is right in my eyes.'"

REFRAINING FROM IDOLATRY

The phrase from the *Shma* "which lead you to act unfaithfully" can be more literally translated "which you prostitute after." The sages saw in this a reference to idolatry, based on Judges 8:33, which refers to Israel's Baal-worship as prostitution.

All these elements included in the prayer are essential in the pursuit of holiness, which is our ultimate goal. Thus, the selection of texts included in the *Shma* is far from arbitrary. Rather, as we recite them, we follow a natural progression of committing our lives to God:

- Acknowledgement of God's oneness
- Love of God
- Learning and teaching about God's ways

- Accepting the responsibility of keeping God's commandments
- Pursuing true holiness

How to Recite the Shma

Get Prepared

Prepare yourself to speak to God with at least as much decorum as you would accord a human noble or king. Find a place that is relatively free of distractions. Be fully dressed, and avoid facing someone who is not fully dressed. Stay away from bad smells.

Make sure that your appearance is respectful. Neaten up your clothes and hair.

You can sit or stand when reciting the *Shma*. Most people sit. (If you are attending a congregation, follow the community custom.)

During the morning (*shacharit*) prayers, some communities have the custom during the *Shma* of holding *tzitziyot* worn on a *tallit* or *tallit katan*. One common method of this is gathering them together, placing them in the left hand between the ring finger and the little finger, and holding them near one's heart. During the third paragraph of the *Shma*, the *tzitziyot* are also grasped with the left hand. (This will be explained later.)

Clear your mind of other thoughts. Think consciously about the fact that you are going to observe the commandment to recite the *Shma*.

"God Is a Faithful King"

If a minyan is not present, recite the introduction: "God is a faithful king." If you are with a minyan, you may skip this line. There are many communities that do not observe the custom of reciting this line at all.

The three paragraphs of the *Shma* consist, in the Hebrew language, of 245 words; including the three Hebrew words that translate "God is a faithful king" brings the total to 248, a number that symbolizes all the parts of the human body. Thus, by including this phrase when praying privately, a person expresses the devotion of his or her entire self to loving God. When praying in a congregation, the cantor repeats three particular words at the end of the prayer.

When praying in English, the number of words is not 248 in any case. Technically, this phrase is only necessary when praying in Hebrew.

In Hebrew, this introductory phrase is *el melech ne'eman* (אֵל מֶלֶךְ נֶאֱמָן). The initial letters of each word of this phrase are *alef* (א), *mem* (מ), and *nun* (נ), which spell *amen*.

"HEAR, O ISRAEL"

Cover the eyes with the right hand while reciting the main line of the *Shma*. This is to block out any distractions and to show that one is not praying to any visible image.

Concentrate on accepting God's kingship. Recite the first line of the *Shma* out loud. State each word clearly while focusing intently on its meaning.

Recite the second line, "Blessed is the name," in a whisper.

"LOVE THE LORD YOUR GOD"

Pause momentarily and concentrate on accepting God's commandments. Be careful not to run the words of this paragraph together. The first paragraph is considered the most essential part of the *Shma*, so make special effort to recite it clearly and with full concentration.

During the morning (*shacharit*) prayers, if you are wearing tefillin, touch the arm tefillin with your fingertips as you say "fasten them to your hand as a sign." When you say "let them be ornaments between your eyes," touch your head tefillin. Then kiss your fingertips.

"IF YOU DUTIFULLY HEED"

Continue to concentrate on accepting God's commandments.

In the morning prayers, when you arrive at "fasten them to your hand as a sign" and "let them be ornaments between your eyes," touch them again as described above.

"THE LORD SAID TO MOSES"

While reciting this prayer, think about the commandment to remember the exodus from Egypt every day.

If you are following the custom of holding the *tzitziyot* during the *Shma*, take hold of the loose ends of the *tzitziyot* with your right hand. Some have the custom of wrapping the tassels once around the pointer finger on each hand. Each time you recite the word "tzitzit" in this passage, kiss the *tzitziyot*. When you recite the words "and you will see them," hold the *tzitziyot* in front of your eyes.

During a more complete prayer service, there is a point shortly after the *Shma* at which the *tzitziyot* are kissed and released. In the highly condensed version of the prayers that we include in Part 3 of this book, you may do this after reciting the *Shma*.

SIDE NOTE:
TOUCHING AND KISSING OBJECTS IN JUDAISM

Some individuals who are unfamiliar with Jewish customs are bothered by the idea of kissing inanimate objects such as tefillin, *tzitziyot*, *mezuzot*, holy books, or Torah scrolls. In Jewish culture kissing an object simply means that one cherishes the item and what it represents. In the case of kissing *tzitziyot*, this simply expresses that the commandment to wear *tzitziyot* as well as all the 613 mitzvot that the *tzitziyot* represent are dear to the person.

Touching the tefillin draws attention to them and helps one maintain focus and awareness about what the prayer is saying. The tefillin are intended to serve as signs, so it makes sense to physically acknowledge them.

THE AMIDAH

The *Amidah* is the central prayer of Judaism. It is so central that Jewish literature often simply refers to it as "the prayer."

The *Amidah* is the high point of the complete prayer service. Each time we pray, it is as though we are ascending through the gates and courts of the heavenly Temple. The prayers leading up to the *Amidah* represent the outer courts; the *Amidah* itself corresponds to the holy of holies. One who has prayed through the service to this point should envision himself standing before the very throne of God, so to speak.

Unlike many of the prayers that are spoken aloud, the *Amidah* is uttered in a mere whisper. This reflects the concept that God is exceptionally close and attentive at this holy moment in the service.

If you were given an audience and allowed to make requests before a mortal ruler, you would seek the king's favor and express the most urgent needs that you and your community face. Likewise, this prayer consists of the most important expressions of praise and prayer in Judaism. Every one of them relates in some way to the Messiah and the final redemption.

"*Amidah*" (עֲמִידָה) literally means "standing." The prayer gets its name from the custom of standing while reciting it, just as people stood when praying in the Temple. Yeshua mentioned this posture of prayer when he said, "Whenever you stand praying, forgive, if you have anything against anyone, so that your Father also who is in heaven may forgive you your trespasses" (Mark 11:25).

Another name for the prayer is *Shmoneh Esreh* (שְׁמֹנֶה עֶשְׂרֵה), which means "eighteen," since it was originally composed of eighteen sections. Today there are nineteen, but this name for the prayer has not changed.

HISTORY OF THE AMIDAH

The history of this prayer is complex. One tradition holds that the *Amidah* was composed by the members of the Great Assembly in the days of Ezra (fifth century BCE).[19] Another version states that Shimon HaPakuli arranged it during the leadership of Rabban Gamliel II (first century CE).[20] The Talmud reconciles this by explaining that although the members of the Great Assembly had composed it long before the first century, the proper sequence of the blessings had been forgotten, and Shimon HaPakuli merely placed them in their proper order.[21]

Some scholars have argued that the name "HaPakuli" (הפקולי) is actually a scribal error and that the name of this sage was actually Shimon Klofi (קלופי)—that is, Simon son of Clopas, one of Yeshua's disciples. If this is true, then Yeshua's followers could have left a dramatic and enduring imprint on Jewish liturgy. For more information on this idea, see D. T. Lancaster's article "Simeon son of Clopas" in *Messiah Journal* 112.

Traces of the *Amidah* and its structure can be found in the books of *2 Maccabees* and *Sirach*, which date to around the second century BCE.

Apostolic Constitutions, a document from the early church, shows that Christians as late as the fourth century CE were still reciting prayers based on the *Amidah*.

STRUCTURE OF THE AMIDAH

The weekday *Amidah* is comprised of nineteen blessings that move along in a natural progression. The first three are considered blessings of praise; the last three are considered blessings of thanks. The thirteen in between are truly petitions, even though they are worded as blessings. On the Sabbath and on holidays, these thirteen petitions are replaced by a single blessing that focuses on the holiness of the day, resulting in a total of seven blessings on those days.

Weekdays	Sabbath and Holidays
Praise (3)	Praise (3)
Petition (13)	Holiness of the day (1)
Thanks (3)	Thanks (3)

The *Amidah* is prayed three times a day on weekdays, with each of the evening, morning, and afternoon prayer services. On the Sabbath and on holidays, the *Amidah* is recited one additional time, which corresponds to the additional burnt offering called the *korban mussaf*.

A person praying alone can pray the *Amidah*, but it is preferable to pray this prayer with a minyan. When a minyan is present, the congregation first prays the *Amidah* silently as individuals, and then the cantor or prayer leader recites it aloud. This is referred to as the "cantor's repetition," or *chazarat shatz* (חזרת ש״ץ).

To pray the *Amidah*:

- Stand and face in the direction of Jerusalem.
- There are certain parts of the prayer that vary on certain days and seasons. Before you start it is good to flip through the text and make a mental note of any special additions or changes for the day.
- Concentrate on the fact that you are entering the presence of the King of the universe.
- Take three steps back, and then take three steps forward. These steps represent moving closer into God's presence.
- Recite the prayer quietly. It should be spoken in a whisper loud enough for you to hear yourself but not loud enough to be heard by others. This quietness reflects the extreme nearness of God and our faith that he hears our prayers.
- At certain specific points it is customary to bow. This is done by first bending the knees, straightening up again, and then bending forward at the waist.

THE THREE BLESSINGS OF PRAISE

According to Jewish thought, one should begin prayer by praising God before offering him petitions.[22] This comes directly from the example of Moses, who requested that he be allowed to enter the land of Israel. Moses prefaced his prayer by saying,

> O Lord GOD, you have only begun to show your servant your greatness and your mighty hand. For what god is there in heaven or on earth who can do such works and mighty acts as yours? (Deuteronomy 3:24)

Only after this praise did he mention his request. Some commentators have even noticed that his words are similar to the first three blessings of the *Amidah*.

Our Master Yeshua also prefaced his prayer with praise: "Our Father, who is in heaven, let your name be sanctified" (Matthew 6:9, Author's translation).

THE FIRST BLESSING:
PRAISE FOR THE PROMISES AND THE COVENANT

> *Blessed are you, O LORD, our God and God of our fathers, the God of Abraham, the God of Isaac, and the God of Jacob, the great, powerful, and fearsome God, God above all, who is generous with kindness and owns all things, who remembers the devotion of the fathers and lovingly brings a redeemer to their descendants for his name's sake. King, helper, savior, and shield! Blessed are you, O LORD, shield of Abraham.*

The first blessing expresses praise for the promises and the covenant. We recognize God as the true and only provider and protector of our people. By reciting this blessing, we open the *Amidah* with the hope of the Messiah by referring to the promised redeemer. Although followers of Yeshua already identify him as the Messiah, we still wait for him to return to redeem the world as God promised he would. With this blessing we declare our trust in God that he will fulfill that promise.

The sages offer explanations as to why each of the blessings of the *Amidah* are arranged in their particular order.[23] We begin our prayer with a blessing that refers to the patriarchs, because Psalm 29 begins, "Ascribe to the LORD, O sons of the mighty" (NASB).

THE SECOND BLESSING:
PRAISE FOR MIRACLES AND RESURRECTION

> *You are powerful forever, my Master. You resurrect the dead, fully able to save. [He sends down the dew/He causes the wind to blow and sends down the rain], with devoted love he sustains those who are living; with deep compassion he resurrects the dead. He upholds those who fall, heals the sick, sets captives free, and maintains his faithfulness to those who sleep in the dust. Who is like you, capable of powerful deeds, and who can compare with you? You are a king who causes death and resurrects, and you make salvation sprout forth! You are faithful to resurrect the dead. Blessed are you, O LORD, who resurrects the dead.*

The second blessing expresses praise for God's all-powerful mastery of his world and for his great miracles, especially the miracle of resurrection. Each of the miracles mentioned (upholding the fallen, healing the sick, and freeing captives) relates to the concept of resurrection in some way. Even the prayers for rain and dew included in this section are connected with resurrection.

Judaism teaches that the dead will be raised to life at the end of the age in connection with the arrival of the Messiah. Rambam included this belief among his "Thirteen Principles," which are considered fundamental to Judaism today.

At the time of Yeshua's earthly ministry, belief in the resurrection was one characteristic that set the Pharisees apart from the Sadducees. As many of the ancient rabbis did, Yeshua quoted the Torah to prove that the dead are raised: "Have you not read what was said to you by God: 'I am the God of Abraham, and the God of Isaac, and the God of Jacob'? He is not God of the dead, but of the living" (Matthew 22:31–32).

The rabbis provided a biblical reason that the mention of God's might follows the blessing regarding the patriarchs: Psalm 29:1 continues, "ascribe to the LORD glory and strength."

THE THIRD BLESSING:
PRAISE FOR THE HOLINESS OF GOD'S NAME

> *You are holy, and your name is holy, and holy ones praise*
> *you every day. Selah. Blessed are you, O LORD, the holy God.*

We reach the absolute pinnacle of the prayer service in the third blessing of the *Amidah*.

The third blessing has two forms. A short form is used during the silent recitation of the *Amidah*, whether one is alone or with a minyan. A longer form is used during the cantor's repetition of the *Amidah* aloud in the presence of a congregation.

The short version used when praying quietly briefly acknowledges God's holiness. It only hints at the angelic worship by saying, "Holy ones praise you every day."

The long version stitches together passages from the Prophets so as to depict the angelic worship constantly being offered before God's throne. These texts speak of the various types of angels, including the *chayot* ("living creatures"), *ofanim* ("wheels"), and *serafim* ("burning ones"), who are calling and responding to one another in worship.

By reciting these passages in unison, the congregation participates in the heavenly liturgy. The prayer begins, "We will sanctify your name in the world as it is sanctified in the highest heights," echoing the words of the *Our Father*: "May your name be sanctified," and, "As your will is done in heaven, so may it also be on earth."

John also caught a glimpse of the angelic liturgy, as he testified in the book of Revelation:

> The four living creatures, each of them with six wings,
> are full of eyes all around and within, and day and night
> they never cease to say, "Holy, holy, holy, is the Lord God
> Almighty, who was and is and is to come!" (Revelation 4:8).

There is a scriptural justification that the blessing regarding the holiness of God's name should follow naturally from the previous two blessings. Psalm 29:2 reads, "Ascribe to the LORD the glory due his name; worship the LORD in the splendor of holiness" (NASB).

THE HOLINESS OF THE SABBATH

As mentioned earlier, on the Sabbath the central portion of the *Amidah* is removed and replaced by one blessing that focuses on the holiness of the Sabbath day.

At each of the four prayer services on the Sabbath (*ma'ariv, shacharit, mussaf,* and *minchah*), this blessing is somewhat different. In our text of the *Amidah* at the end of this book, we have simplified the prayer so that it contains only the core part that remains the same for each service.

THE THIRTEEN WEEKDAY PETITIONS

The thirteen blessings at the center of the *Amidah* (which are actually petitions) are omitted on the Sabbath and on holidays.

On the surface most of the requests seem to be for something relatively mundane, such as healing or forgiveness—things that we need every day in this world. But in the larger context, one can see that each prayer is related to the ultimate redemption, the coming of the Messiah, and the onset of the Messianic Era.

Accordingly, the requests find parallels in the prophecies about the process of redemption in the Scriptures. Two passages that are foundational to understanding the redemption are Deuteronomy 30 and Jeremiah 30–31, and additional parallels can be found throughout the biblical prophecies. Thus, as we read through each blessing of the petition section of the *Amidah*, we will find that the petitions echo the promises of the new covenant described in these chapters of Deuteronomy and Jeremiah.

Each petition is thus a prayer for another step in the Messianic redemption process to occur, arranged logically (not necessarily chronologically).

THE FOURTH BLESSING:
PRAYER FOR DISCERNMENT

> *You bestow knowledge to humans and teach mortals discernment. Grant us knowledge, discernment, and understanding from you. Blessed are you, O LORD, who bestows knowledge.*

On weekdays the section of petitions begins with a prayer for discernment. Discernment (*binah*) in Jewish thought represents the ability to perceive proper distinctions, such as the difference between holy and common, clean and unclean, permitted and forbidden, blessing and curse.

This parallels the beginning of Deuteronomy 30, in which God promises when the redemption will begin: "When all these things come upon you, the blessing and the curse, which I have set before you, and you call them to mind among all the nations where the LORD your God has driven you" (Deuteronomy 30:1).

An increase of knowledge and understanding also corresponds to the increased awareness of God that will characterize the Messianic Era:

> No longer shall each one teach his neighbor and each his brother, saying, "Know the LORD," for they shall all know me, from the least of them to the greatest, declares the LORD. (Jeremiah 31:34)

The sages of the Talmud provide a biblical reason that a prayer for discernment naturally follows a declaration for the holiness of God: Isaiah 29:23 reads, "They will sanctify the Holy One of Jacob and will stand in awe of the God of Israel." The next verse says, "And those who go astray in spirit will come to understanding [Hebrew: *binah*]."

THE FIFTH BLESSING:
PRAYER FOR REPENTANCE

> *Return us, our Father, to your Torah. Draw us near, our King, to your service, and help us to return to you in complete repentance. Blessed are you, O LORD, who desires repentance.*

The fifth blessing is not a prayer of repentance but a prayer *for* repentance—that we and all Israel would be granted the desire and strength to repent.

Repentance is closely connected to the Messianic Kingdom; it is central to the message of good news that Yeshua taught. The Gospels record that Yeshua proclaimed, "The time is fulfilled, and the kingdom of God is at hand; repent and believe in the gospel" (Mark 1:14–15).

Repentance naturally follows discernment, the awareness of right and wrong. Repentance in Hebrew is *teshuvah* (תְּשׁוּבָה), which literally means "returning."

Deuteronomy 30 and Jeremiah 31 explain that repentance would follow the people calling to mind the blessing and curse:

> Return to the LORD your God, you and your children, and obey his voice in all that I command you today, with all your heart and with all your soul. (Deuteronomy 30:2)

> I have heard Ephraim grieving, "You have disciplined me, and I was disciplined, like an untrained calf; bring me back that I may be restored, for you are the LORD my God. For after I had turned away, I relented, and after I was instructed, I struck my thigh; I was ashamed, and I was confounded, because I bore the disgrace of my youth." (Jeremiah 31:18–19)

The sages reasoned that the prayer for repentance should follow the prayer for discernment based on the process described in Isaiah 6:10: "[The people] understand with their hearts, and turn [i.e., repent] and [are] healed." (The sages note that "healing" in this verse refers to forgiveness rather than physical healing.)

THE SIXTH BLESSING:
PRAYER FOR FORGIVENESS

> *Forgive us, our Father, for we have sinned. Pardon us, our King, for we have transgressed. For you pardon and forgive. Blessed are you, O LORD, abundantly gracious to forgive.*

This petition acknowledges sin and pleads for forgiveness and pardon. This step in the redemption process follows naturally from repentance.

Obtaining forgiveness for mankind's sin was a main task of Yeshua's ministry, and this task is closely connected to the redemption, which will be the fulfillment of the promises of the new covenant:

He took a cup, and when he had given thanks he gave it to them, saying, "Drink of it, all of you, for this is my blood of the covenant, which is poured out for many for the forgiveness of sins. I tell you I will not drink again of this fruit of the vine until that day when I drink it new with you in my Father's kingdom." (Matthew 26:27–29)

We find forgiveness likewise mentioned in the prophecies of the Messianic process. Moses promised, "The LORD your God will restore your fortunes and have mercy on you" (Deuteronomy 30:3). Jeremiah explains regarding the new covenant, "I will forgive their iniquity, and I will remember their sin no more" (Jeremiah 31:34).

THE SEVENTH BLESSING:
PRAYER FOR REDEMPTION

Take note of our suffering, and take on our struggle, and quickly redeem us for the sake of your name, because you are a strong redeemer. Blessed are you, O LORD, the redeemer of Israel.

Redemption is the return of something to its rightful or original owner, often by its being literally or figuratively bought back: "The LORD has ransomed Jacob and has redeemed him from hands too strong for him." (Jeremiah 31:11)

The words of the prayer "take note of our suffering" mean that we desire God to notice with concern that things are not the way they ought to be. By saying "take on our struggle," we express that we want God to fight for us on our behalf to bring redemption. In the immediate sense we ask that God would intervene in our personal and community affairs, in areas where we have to deal with courts and governments, and in other situations that may not always be in our favor. But with a view to the ultimate redemption, we desire God to free the world from the bonds of tyranny, secularism, and other religions.

Slaves are redeemed when they are freed from captivity, such as when the Israelites were saved from slavery in Egypt. The current exile is also compared to slavery, and so the future redemption parallels the exodus from Egypt:

It shall come to pass in that day, declares the LORD of hosts, that I will break his yoke from off your neck, and I will burst your bonds, and foreigners shall no more make a servant of him (Jeremiah 30:8).

The reason that the ancient scholars gave for listing the blessing for redemption as the seventh one is more symbolic than scriptural. Seven is a number that represents redemption, and in the view of the sages, the Messiah will come after a tumultuous seven-year period called "the footsteps of Messiah."[24] Thus, it is fitting that redemption is the focus of the seventh blessing.

THE EIGHTH BLESSING:
PRAYER FOR HEALING

Heal us, O LORD, and we will be healed; save us and we will be saved, for you are our praise. Bring about complete healing for all our ailments.

For you, God and King, are a faithful and compassionate healer. Blessed are you, O LORD, healer of the sick among his people Israel.

In this prayer we pray for the sick and injured. During this prayer it is appropriate to pause and mention the specific names of individuals in need of healing. We ask not only for their bodily recovery but for spiritual healing as well. After all, the verse that says "Heal me, O LORD, and I shall be healed" (Jeremiah 17:14) speaks in context about spiritual restoration.

Healing in this world is really only treating the symptom. The true source of all suffering is the fallen state of mankind. For true healing to come, the world must be repaired. This is an essential step in the ultimate redemption process. "I will restore health to you, and your wounds I will heal, declares the LORD" (Jeremiah 30:17).

One aspect of this spiritual healing is the correction of our faulty inward desires that lead us away from God. Followers of Yeshua who have become a "new creation" have seen the beginning of this process, but there is more work to be done:

> The LORD your God will circumcise your heart and the heart of your offspring, so that you will love the LORD your God with all your heart and with all your soul, that you may live. (Deuteronomy 30:6)

Yeshua's ministry naturally involved both spiritual and physical healing as he proclaimed the kingdom. His followers applied the verse to him that says, "Upon him was the chastisement that brought us peace, and with his wounds we are healed" (Isaiah 53:5).

Due to the overriding significance of the number seven, the previous blessing of redemption interposed in the logical process of the prayers. However, this eighth blessing for healing is logically the next stage in the process after forgiveness, the sixth blessing. Psalm 103:2–3 says, "The LORD … forgives all your iniquity [and] heals all your diseases." Furthermore, as with the blessing for redemption, the sages placed the blessing for healing as the eighth for a symbolic reason. The number eight corresponds to the day when a child is circumcised and requires healing.

THE NINTH BLESSING:
PRAYER FOR HARVEST

> *Bless this year for us, O LORD our God, and bless all its types of produce with goodness. [Send a blessing/Send dew and rain for a blessing] upon the face of the land. Satisfy us with your goodness, and bless this year as one of the best years. Blessed are you, O LORD, who blesses the years.*

Each year we hope for and rely on abundant crops as well as for success in other financial endeavors. Not only do we pray for abundance in our lands and in the land of Israel, but we also look forward to the "best years": the Messianic Era.

Deuteronomy 30 describes the Messianic future: "The LORD your God will make you abundantly prosperous in all the work of your hand, in the fruit of your womb and in the fruit of your cattle and in the fruit of your ground" (Deuteronomy 30:9).

Jeremiah describes this in detail:

> They shall come and sing aloud on the height of Zion,
> and they shall be radiant over the goodness of the LORD,

over the grain, the wine, and the oil, and over the young of the flock and the herd; their life shall be like a watered garden, and they shall languish no more. Then shall the young women rejoice in the dance, and the young men and the old shall be merry. I will turn their mourning into joy; I will comfort them, and give them gladness for sorrow. I will feast the soul of the priests with abundance, and my people shall be satisfied with my goodness, declares the LORD. (Jeremiah 31:12–14)

The Messianic Era is a step toward an Edenic state of blessing and abundance. Jewish literature describes the fruitfulness of the Messianic future in hyperbolic terms.

A church tradition records that Yeshua spoke also of the Messianic future as a time of plentiful harvest:

> The elders who saw John, the disciple of the Master, remembered that they had heard from him how the Master taught concerning those times, and said: "The days will come in which vineyards shall grow, each one possessing ten thousand vines, and each vine will have ten thousand branches, and on every branch will be ten thousand shoots, and from each one of the shoots ten thousand clusters will grow, and from every one of the clusters ten thousand grapes, and every grape will produce twenty-five measures of wine in the press. And when any one of the righteous takes hold of a single cluster, another will cry out, 'Taste me! My springs are richer than wine. I am a better cluster, take me, bless the LORD through me.'"

> In like manner, he said that "a single grain of wheat will produce ten thousand ears, and every ear will have ten thousand grains, and every grain will yield ten pounds of clear, pure, fine flour. Likewise, all other fruits and seeds and vegetation will bring forth in similar proportions, and all the animals, feeding then only on the products of the earth, will become peaceful and docile, and live in willing subjugation to humans." [25]

The sages' reasoning for placing this blessing in the ninth position is admittedly a little tenuous. The sages interpret Psalm 10 as condemning the practice of inflating food prices. With an abundance of food in the Messianic Era, however, it will not be possible to do so. The psalms were numbered differently in ancient times, so Psalm 10 was counted as Psalm 9—hence the prayer for the harvest as the ninth blessing.

THE TENTH BLESSING:
PRAYER FOR GATHERING OF THE EXILES

> *Blast the great shofar for our freedom. Lift a banner to gather our exiles, and gather us together from the four corners of the earth. Blessed are you, O LORD, who gathers those who are scattered of his people Israel.*

The ingathering is one of the most prominent promises of the Messianic Era. The Scriptures promise that Israel will be gathered from exile, from the extremities of the earth, and miraculously placed in the land of Israel:

> He will gather you again from all the peoples where the LORD your God has scattered you. If your outcasts are in the uttermost parts of heaven, from there the LORD your God will gather you, and from there he will take you." (Deuteronomy 30:3–4)

> Behold, days are coming, declares the LORD, when I will restore the fortunes of my people, Israel and Judah, says the LORD, and I will bring them back to the land that I gave to their fathers, and they shall take possession of it. (Jeremiah 30:3)

> Hear the word of the LORD, O nations, and declare it in the coastlands far away; say, "He who scattered Israel will gather him, and will keep him as a shepherd keeps his flock." (Jeremiah 31:10)

The Messiah spoke of this event when he said, "He will send out his angels with a loud trumpet call, and they will gather his elect from the four winds, from one end of heaven to the other" (Matthew 24:31).

The sages explained that the blessing for the ingathering follows the blessing for the harvest based on Ezekiel 36:8: "But you, O mountains of Israel, shall shoot forth your branches and yield your fruit to my people Israel, for they will soon come home."

THE ELEVENTH BLESSING: PRAYER FOR JUSTICE

> *Restore our judges as at first and our counselors as in the beginning. Take away our grief and groaning, and reign over us—you, O LORD, alone—with devotion and with compassion, vindicating us with justice. Blessed are you, O LORD, King who loves righteousness and justice.*

This is a prayer that Israel will have sovereignty, without another kingdom or empire ruling over it, and that the judges who rule over Israel will be righteous and enforce Torah law. The Torah and the Prophets predicted this as a part of the redemption:

> The LORD will again take delight in prospering you, as he took delight in your fathers, when you obey the voice of the LORD your God, to keep his commandments and his statutes that are written in this Book of the Law, when you turn to the LORD your God with all your heart and with all your soul. (Deuteronomy 30:9–10)

> Jacob shall return and have quiet and ease, and none shall make him afraid. (Jeremiah 30:10)

The sages connect the ingathering with the establishment of justice, based on Isaiah 1:25–26:

> I will turn my hand against you and will smelt away your dross as with lye and remove all your alloy. And I will restore your judges as at the first, and your counselors as at the beginning.

THE TWELFTH BLESSING:
PRAYER FOR PUNISHMENT OF THE WICKED

> *Let there be no hope for the slanderers, and may you*
> *instantly destroy all wickedness. Let all your enemies be*
> *swiftly cut down, and may you swiftly uproot, shatter,*
> *throw down, and humble the arrogant offenders, soon and*
> *during our lives. Blessed are you, O LORD, who smashes*
> *enemies and humbles the arrogant.*

The twelfth blessing is quite often misunderstood. It has a complex and remarkable history.

The prayer asks for retribution against those who have harmed or attacked Israel. Judgment against Israel's enemies is one of the promises of the Messianic redemption, so the request is in keeping with the other petitions in this section of the *Amidah*:

> The LORD your God will put all these curses on your foes
> and enemies who persecuted you. (Deuteronomy 30:7)

> I am with you to save you, declares the LORD; I will make
> a full end of all the nations among whom I scattered you,
> but of you I will not make a full end. (Jeremiah 30:11)

> Therefore all who devour you shall be devoured, and all
> your foes, every one of them, shall go into captivity; those
> who plunder you shall be plundered, and all who prey
> on you I will make a prey. (Jeremiah 30:16)

This vengeance is so important that it is to be carried out by none other than the Messiah himself:

> Who is this who comes from Edom, in crimsoned gar-
> ments from Bozrah, he who is splendid in his apparel,
> marching in the greatness of his strength? "It is I, speaking
> in righteousness, mighty to save." Why is your apparel
> red, and your garments like his who treads in the wine-
> press? "I have trodden the winepress alone, and from the
> peoples no one was with me; I trod them in my anger and
> trampled them in my wrath; their lifeblood spattered on
> my garments, and stained all my apparel. For the day of

vengeance was in my heart, and my year of redemption had come." (Isaiah 63:1–4)

Even today Israel has many enemies. When the Messiah comes, he will vanquish them. Thus, to pray for judgment against Israel's enemies is to pray for the Messiah to come.

For followers of Yeshua, this prayer has its difficulties. Over the course of centuries, the wording of the prayer has changed frequently.

Based on an anecdote from the Talmud,[26] it is sometimes taught that this prayer was originally composed at Yavneh after the destruction of the Temple specifically in order to separate followers of Yeshua from the Jewish community. It certainly was used this way at times, but the event described in this anecdote must be describing a redaction or modification of the prayer rather than its original composition.

Other than the initial mention of the "slanderers," it sounds as though the prayer is mainly directed toward an oppressive occupying empire, such as the pre-Christian Romans or the Syrians. This may suggest that the original version of the prayer was directed more generally against hostile nations rather than sectarians within Judaism.

The modification at Yavneh might have been to add a specific curse against wicked individuals. As tensions grew between mainstream Judaism and sectarian groups (including not only various groups of believers in Yeshua but also Sadducees, Samaritans, and gnostics), the terms used in the prayer changed to specifically identify the offenders. Some versions of the prayer actually used the term *Notzrim* ("Nazarenes" or "Christians") as well as *meshumadim*, which is a derogatory term for someone who used to practice Judaism or was born Jewish but converted to another religion.

A common misconception is that this is the blessing that brought the total number in the *Amidah* from eighteen to nineteen. Rather, the blessing for the restoration of the Davidic kingship and the prayer for the rebuilding of Jerusalem were originally combined into one unit. When they eventually split, the number of blessings increased from eighteen to nineteen.

What about our Master's instruction, "Love your enemies and pray for those who persecute you" (Matthew 5:44; see also Luke 6:27)? One might suppose that this teaching contradicts the practice of reciting the blessing for the punishment of the wicked. However, Yeshua's words do not concern foreign powers or religions that attack the Jewish people. Rather, he was trying to forge interpersonal unity among the Jewish people and to mend broken relationships.

In this prayer we are not speaking of our own enemies or people with whom we have vendettas and quarrels but rather of the enemies of God. These are not the people who threaten us personally but those who threaten the existence of Israel and godliness as a whole. While we pray for wicked individuals to repent and be reconciled to God, Scripture is clear that the wicked in general will be punished and thwarted.

Just as the sages connected the blessing for justice with Isaiah 1:25–26, so they reasoned that the punishment of the wicked should follow, according to Isaiah 1:28: "But rebels and sinners shall be broken together, and those who forsake the LORD shall be consumed."

THE THIRTEENTH BLESSING:
PRAYER FOR THE RIGHTEOUS

> *On behalf of the righteous, the devout, and the elders of your people, the house of Israel, the scholars who remain, the righteous converts, and on our behalf may your compassion be incited, O LORD our God. Give a good reward to all those who truly trust in your name. Place our share with them forever so that we will not be put to shame, for we trust in you. Blessed are you, O LORD, the support and security for the righteous.*

In the future redemption those who have remained faithful will receive their reward. This is hinted at in Moses' words:

> If you obey the commandments of the LORD your God that I command you today, by loving the LORD your God, by walking in his ways, and by keeping his command-

ments and his statutes and his rules, then you shall live
and multiply. (Deuteronomy 30:16)

Yeshua's teachings about reward frequently follow the principle
that those who fail to receive the reward they deserve in this world
will receive it in the future. This includes those who are persecuted
in this life: "Rejoice and be glad, for your reward is great in heaven,
for so they persecuted the prophets who were before you" (Matthew 5:12).

(When he says that the reward is "in heaven," Yeshua does
not mean that it is awaiting individuals for when they arrive in
heaven but that it is saved up with God to be bestowed on earth
at the proper time.)

Those who "love [their] enemies, and do good, … expecting
nothing in return" also receive a reward (Luke 6:35). Yeshua speaks
too about how one might lose (or fail to gain) his reward, including
by loving only those who love him (Matthew 5:46) or by practicing
acts of righteousness in order to be seen by others (Matthew
6:1–18), since one who does this has already received his reward.

Yeshua taught that not only do the righteous receive a reward
but so also do those who receive, support, and show kindness to
them:

> The one who receives a prophet because he is a prophet
> will receive a prophet's reward, and the one who receives
> a righteous person because he is a righteous person will
> receive a righteous person's reward. And whoever gives
> one of these little ones even a cup of cold water because
> he is a disciple, truly, I say to you, he will by no means
> lose his reward. (Matthew 10:41–42)

When we pray for the righteous to be rewarded, we are praying
for the fullness of the Messianic Era to come.

The basis for seeking the blessing of the righteous immediately
after mentioning the punishment of the wicked is Psalm 75:11[10]:
"All the horns of the wicked I will cut off, but the horns of the righteous shall be lifted up."

THE FOURTEENTH BLESSING:
PRAYER FOR THE REBUILDING OF JERUSALEM

> *Return to Jerusalem, your city, with compassion, and dwell*
> *in its midst as you have said. Build it, soon and during*
> *our lives, as an eternal structure. And establish the throne*
> *of David within it. Blessed are you, O LORD, who builds*
> *Jerusalem.*

One of the promises of the new covenant is that Jerusalem will be rebuilt, never to be destroyed again:

> Thus says the LORD: Behold, I will restore the fortunes of
> the tents of Jacob and have compassion on his dwellings;
> the city shall be rebuilt on its mound, and the palace shall
> stand where it used to be. (Jeremiah 30:18)

> Behold, the days are coming, declares the LORD, when
> the city shall be rebuilt for the LORD from the Tower of
> Hananel to the Corner Gate. And the measuring line shall
> go out farther, straight to the hill Gareb, and shall then
> turn to Goah. The whole valley of the dead bodies and the
> ashes, and all the fields as far as the brook Kidron, to the
> corner of the Horse Gate toward the east, shall be sacred
> to the LORD. It shall not be plucked up or overthrown
> anymore forever. (Jeremiah 31:38–40)

This promise refers to Messianic Jerusalem, which will be the capital city of the entire world when King Messiah rules and the Torah goes forth from Zion. The promise will find its ultimate fulfillment when the New Jerusalem descends from heaven (Revelation 3:12, 21:2). In the meantime, we also pray for present-day Jerusalem's peace and security.

The prayer for the restoration of Jerusalem follows the blessing of the righteous, since the righteous will be blessed in Jerusalem. Psalm 122:6 says, "Pray for the peace of Jerusalem! May they be secure who love you!"

THE FIFTEENTH BLESSING:
PRAYER FOR RESTORATION OF DAVIDIC KINGSHIP

Cause the Branch of David your servant to sprout forth swiftly, whose horn will be raised with your salvation, for we hope for your salvation all day long. Blessed are you, O LORD, who causes the horn of salvation to sprout forth.

God promised David that the kingship rightfully belonged to his descendants forever (2 Samuel 7:16). But since the Babylonian exile, no Davidic king has ruled over Israel. The restoration of all things will include restoring David's offspring to the throne. This will happen when Messiah, the Son of David, reigns as King:

Their prince shall be one of themselves; their ruler shall come out from their midst; I will make him draw near, and he shall approach me, for who would dare of himself to approach me? declares the LORD. (Jeremiah 30:21)

In Ezekiel's prophecy God refers to the Messiah as "David":

My servant David shall be king over them, and they shall all have one shepherd. They shall walk in my rules and be careful to obey my statutes. They shall dwell in the land that I gave to my servant Jacob, where your fathers lived. They and their children and their children's children shall dwell there forever, and David my servant shall be their prince forever. (Ezekiel 37:24–25)

Yehudah Liebes, professor of Jewish mysticism and Kabbalah in the department of Jewish thought at the Hebrew University of Jerusalem, asserted that the original conclusion of this blessing was the phrase "who causes a horn for David to sprout forth" (*matzmiach keren ledavid*, מַצְמִיחַ קֶרֶן לְדָוִד). He explained that the version we use today, which states "who causes the horn of salvation to sprout forth" (*matzmiach keren yeshu'ah*, מַצְמִיחַ קֶרֶן יְשׁוּעָה), was formulated by early Jewish followers of Yeshua, who alluded to his name in the prayer.

The prayer for Messiah should follow that of the building of Jerusalem, because according to the sages, "once Jerusalem is built, the Son of David will come." They cite Hosea 3:5 as proof:

"Afterward the children of Israel shall return [to the Temple] and seek the LORD their God, and David their king."

THE SIXTEENTH BLESSING:
PRAYER FOR ACCEPTANCE

Hear our voice, O LORD our God. Take pity and have compassion on us, and accept our prayer with compassion and favor. Our King, do not turn us away from your presence empty handed! For you hear the prayer of every mouth. Blessed are you, O LORD, who hears prayer.

The final prayer in the section of weekday petitions is a plea for compassion and favor. It asks that God will not be like the unrighteous judge who was bothered by the obnoxious voice of the claimant but that our voice will move him to true compassion.

It was the sound of the pleas of Israel that led to the nation's redemption from Egypt:

> We cried to the LORD, the God of our fathers, and the LORD heard our voice and saw our affliction, our toil, and our oppression. (Deuteronomy 26:7)

> During those many days the king of Egypt died, and the people of Israel groaned because of their slavery and cried out for help. Their cry for rescue from slavery came up to God. (Exodus 2:23)

Similar imagery appears in Jeremiah 31, as Rachel is pictured mourning over the exile:

> Thus says the LORD: "A voice is heard in Ramah, lamentation and bitter weeping. Rachel is weeping for her children; she refuses to be comforted for her children, because they are no more." Thus says the LORD: "Keep your voice from weeping, and your eyes from tears, for there is a reward for your work, declares the LORD, and they shall come back from the land of the enemy. (Jeremiah 31:14–15[15–16])

Based on the verse, "These I will bring to my holy mountain, and make them joyful in my house of prayer" (Isaiah 56:7), the rabbis deduced that the blessing for the acceptance of prayer should follow the blessing for Davidic kingship. The sages operate on the principle that the Temple will be built only after the king is appointed. Thus, the presence of the Temple in this verse implies the prior inauguration of the Messiah king.

The Three Blessings of Thanks

The final three blessings of the *Amidah* relate to giving thanks. At the same time, they also express additional requests.

The Hebrew word for "thank" also means "to admit." By thanking someone we admit and acknowledge that he or she has helped us in some way. With God we admit and acknowledge that we are utterly reliant on him; our requests in this section express our awareness that everything we have comes from him. Thus, these petitions actually serve to thank God for what he has done and will do for us.

THE SEVENTEENTH BLESSING:
THANKSGIVING FOR THE TEMPLE SERVICE

> *Show favor to your people Israel and their prayer, O LORD, our God, and bring back the service to the inner chamber of your house. May you favorably accept the fire offerings of Israel and their loving prayer, and may the service of your people Israel always be favorable.*
>
> *Let our eyes behold your compassionate return to Zion. Blessed are you, O LORD, who is bringing back his Dwelling Presence to Zion.*

The first blessing of thanks is a prayer that the Temple service will return. That means that we pray for priests descended from Aaron to resume their duties in the rebuilt house of God, bringing offerings and performing other duties.

When the Temple was still standing, this prayer was worded differently. Rather than asking God to restore the Temple service, it simply asked him to accept the Temple offerings with favor.

People from a Christian background may raise an eyebrow at this. How can we ask for the Temple service to be restored as before, considering that Jesus is our sacrifice once for all (Hebrews 10:10)?

However, the epistle to the Hebrews is often misunderstood. Its writer explains that there are two sanctuaries: the earthly Sanctuary and the heavenly Sanctuary. There is a contrast between the two. Yeshua's sacrifice and priestly ministry operate exclusively in the realm of the heavenly Sanctuary. In the earthly Sanctuary he does not qualify as either a priest or a sacrifice. The function of the heavenly Sanctuary is in regard to eternal life and the World to Come. The earthly Sanctuary and the atonement secured there is limited in scope to this world and to meeting with God in the physical Temple.

When Yeshua secured atonement for us in the World to Come, he accomplished something magnificent and that has enormous significance. However, it applies only in the heavenly Tabernacle and in that future world. Until that world is fully realized, the same rules continue to apply in a physical, earthly Temple. That is why the believers who met in the Temple in Jerusalem continued to participate in the sacrificial system.

The Prophets teach that sacrifices will once again be offered in the Messianic Era. The prophet Malachi describes how Israel will be purified when the Messiah comes:

> He will sit as a refiner and purifier of silver, and he will purify the sons of Levi and refine them like gold and silver, and they will bring offerings in righteousness to the LORD. Then the offering of Judah and Jerusalem will be pleasing to the LORD as in the days of old and as in former years. (Malachi 3:3–4)

Since the Temple services will resume when Yeshua returns, by praying for the services to resume, we are praying for his coming.

THE EIGHTEENTH BLESSING:
THANKSGIVING FOR GOD'S GOODNESS

> *We are thankful that you, O LORD, are our God and God of our fathers forever and ever. You are the rock of our lives, the shield of our salvation in every generation. We*

*will give thanks to you and praise you for our lives that
are placed in your care, for our souls that are under your
protection, for your miracles that are with us daily, and
for your incomprehensible acts of goodness that happen
all the time: evening, morning, and afternoon. We call you
"good" because your compassions never stop and "compassionate" because your kindness never ends. Since long ago
we have hoped in you.*

*For all these things, may your name be blessed and lifted
up, our King, continually and forever and ever. Every living
thing will acknowledge you. Selah. They will truly praise
your name, the God of our salvation and our help. Selah.
Blessed are you, O LORD; "Good" is your name, and it is
fitting to thank you.*

The way to say "thank you" in Hebrew is *todah* (תּוֹדָה). This word
also means "admission," "acknowledgement," or "confession."
To thank someone means to admit, acknowledge, or confess that
one has benefitted from or relied upon him or her in some way.
This blessing acknowledges that our very souls and everything
we have comes from God.

God's miracles, the *Amidah* states, are "with us daily." This
refers not just to the big miracles that seem to violate the laws of
nature. Since everything comes from God, miracles are constant.
We need only be perceptive enough to see them.

One of the sacrifices that was offered in the Temple was the
thank offering, or in Hebrew, the *korban todah* (קָרְבַּן תּוֹדָה). A person
offered this sacrifice in response to an act of salvation, such as
being enabled to cross a desert or the sea safely, being released
from prison, or being healed from a life-threatening illness (see
Psalm 107).

Giving thanks is closely linked in Scripture to the thank offering. The sages thus saw it fit to connect the prayer for the Temple
services to the prayer of thanksgiving.

The final line of this blessing is, "Good is your name, and it is
fitting to thank you." This is reminiscent of Yeshua's statement that
"no one is good except God alone" (Mark 10:18; Luke 18:19; see also
Matthew 19:17). However, the original version of this blessing read

hatov lecha lehodot (הַטּוֹב לְךָ לְהוֹדוֹת), which means "to whom it is good to give thanks," echoing the words of Psalm 92:2[1].

THE PRIESTLY BLESSING AND THE NINETEENTH BLESSING: THANKSGIVING FOR PEACE

> *Our God and God of our fathers, bless us with the threefold blessing in the Torah, which was written by your servant Moses, pronounced by Aaron and his sons, the priests, your holy people, as it is said:*
>
> *May the LORD bless you and protect you.*
>
> *May the LORD shine his face upon you and be gracious to you.*
>
> *May the LORD lift his face to you and grant peace to you.*

One of the most well-known Hebrew words is *shalom* (שָׁלוֹם). This word is often translated "peace," but it also signifies wholeness and well-being. It denotes completeness and the fulfillment of anything lacking.

Shalom is precious to Judaism. That is why it is used as a greeting. Based on Judges 6:24, the rabbis even considered it to be one of the names of God.[27] For this reason, we do not use the word "shalom" to greet someone in the restroom, as it is not befitting God's dignity.

While Judaism acknowledges the existence of good and evil, right and wrong, the positive and negative components of this world are more commonly viewed in terms of "whole" and "broken." What others sometimes describe as good triumphing over evil, Judaism tends to describe as rectification and perfection of what is flawed or incomplete. This fundamentally affects the way we address problems in the world, big or small.

The goal of redemption, both on a personal level and on a global level, is true shalom.

The priestly blessing, from Numbers 6:24–26, illustrates the supreme objective of peace. God instructed the descendants of Aaron (the *kohanim)* to pronounce this blessing. In Temple times it was recited every day by the *kohanim*, and this is still the case in many Israeli synagogues. In synagogues outside the land of Israel, the *kohanim* pronounce this blessing over the congregation only on holidays. When a *kohen* recites the blessing, the people respond with "amen," affirming its words.

A cantor who is not a *kohen* does not actually recite this blessing directly. Instead of speaking the words of blessing over the congregation (a privilege reserved for the *kohanim*), he offers a prayer asking God to bless the congregation. Instead of saying "amen," the congregation responds with "let this be his will," thus joining the cantor in his prayer.

The priestly blessing section is only added to the *Amidah* when one is praying in a congregation and only during the morning service (*shacharit*). On fast days it is also included in the afternoon (*minchah*).

The words of the priestly blessing beautifully relate the promises of the new covenant. Many echoes of this blessing can be found in Jeremiah 31:

- "May the LORD bless you." This refers to material blessings and success in each person's endeavors (Jeremiah 31:23).

- "And protect you." The more wealth and success a person has, the more enemies he has. Let God not only grant blessing to his people but also keep them safe (Jeremiah 31:28).

- "May the LORD shine his face upon you." "Illumination" is an idiom for divine revelation and the knowledge of God's will. We ask that God reveal himself to us through understanding the depths of the Torah (Jeremiah 31:33–34).

- "And be gracious to you." The revelation of God and his Torah is a dangerous thing. When God is revealed, the righteous are rewarded, and the wicked are punished. At the same time, we desire God's revelation, and we ask that it take the form of grace and that God look upon us with favor (Jeremiah 31:34).

- "May the LORD lift his face to you." When a person "lifts his face" toward someone, it means that he gives that person special treatment. God may not show favoritism in the sense of justice, but he does choose whom he will choose. So we ask that God will elevate the status of Israel in a practical way on earth such that it is recognized by other nations (Jeremiah 31:36–37).

- "And grant peace to you." Chosen-ness comes with troubles, particularly when those who are chosen interact with those who are not. That is why the blessing concludes with "and give you peace." This refers to the peace between Israel and all nations as Israel acknowledges God's special selection of them (Jeremiah 31:38–40).

When *kohanim* recite this blessing, they lift their hands and place their fingers in a way that resembles the ancient shape of the Hebrew letter *shin* (ש) which originally looked more like a modern 'W'. Based on this, the recital of the priestly blessing is sometimes called "Lifting the Hands," or in Hebrew, *nesi'at kappayim* (נְשִׂיאַת כַּפַּיִם).

This is the blessing that Yeshua pronounced as he ascended to heaven. As Luke relates, "He led them out as far as Bethany, and lifting up his hands he blessed them" (Luke 24:50). This alludes to Leviticus 9:22: "Then Aaron lifted up his hands toward the people and blessed them."

OUR FATHER

Our Father, who is in heaven,
let your name be sanctified;
let your kingdom come;
let your will be done—as in heaven, so on earth.

Give us today our bread of tomorrow,
and pardon our debts,
as we also have pardoned those indebted to us,
and do not let us be overcome by trials,
but rescue us from what is evil.

For yours is the kingdom and the power
and the majesty, forever and ever. Amen.

For the sake of our Master Yeshua, in his merit
and virtues, may the sayings of my mouth and the
meditation of my heart be favorable before you,
O LORD, my rock and my redeemer.

Yeshua's disciples asked him how to pray, and he gave them a very direct and clear response. As it did for his disciples, his prayer, *Our Father*, should occupy a central place in our prayer life.

The Gospels record two versions of this prayer, one in Matthew 6:9–13 and another in Luke 11:2–4. Most scholars suppose that Luke's version is the most original, since it is shorter and simpler than the one in Matthew; liturgical text tends to expand over time. Some, including Brad Young and Geza Vermes, feel that Matthew's is closer to the original and that Luke simplified it out of concern for his readership.

Looking at it from a Jewish perspective, however, we need not be bothered by the fact that this prayer appears in two versions, nor do we need to choose one and discard the other. Both *nusachim* (traditional wordings) are a part of the *mesorah* (handed-down tradition) of our community, so we should embrace both.

Many scholars note the similarity of *Our Father* to traditional Jewish prayers, sometimes playing a game of "which came first?" The most common comparisons are to the *Amidah* and to *Kaddish*. However, every line of *Our Father* can be compared to a similar passage in the traditional Siddur.

While Orthodox Jews who do not follow Yeshua would feel uncomfortable with saying this prayer because of its association with Christianity, there is nothing inherently Christian about it. As to its individual petitions and expressions, any Orthodox Jewish person would agree.

The *Didache* contains this prayer in a version that is quite similar to that of Matthew, and it instructs believers to recite it three times a day. From the earliest available records, Christians have used this prayer as a part of liturgical worship. Like a majority of traditional Jewish prayers, the first-person pronouns in *Our Father* are plural ("us," "our"). This suggests that the prayer was intended for corporate liturgical use.

Some scholars see *Our Father* as a version of the *Amidah*, based on its structure as well as its liturgical use three times a day. However, this is quite unlikely. Its brief contents do not generally match those of the *Amidah*. Even its structure is not very similar, especially considering that the doxology at the end does not appear in the most reliable manuscripts and was probably not a part of the original prayer.

Rabbinic literature records a few examples of brief prayers that one can say when traveling or in danger as an alternative to the *Amidah*:

> Rabbi Yehoshua says: One who is traveling in a dangerous place may offer a brief prayer, saying, "Save, O LORD, your people, the remnant of Israel. At every crossing, let their needs be before you. Blessed are you, O LORD, who hears prayer."[28]

One who is traveling in a place of danger or bandits may offer a brief prayer. What is a brief prayer?

- Rabbi Elazar says, "Do your will in heaven, give relief to those who fear you on earth, and do what is good in your sight. Blessed is the one who hears prayer."
- Rabbi Elazar bar Tzadok says, "Hear the cry of your people Israel, and quickly fulfill their request. Blessed is the one who hears prayer."
- Others say, "The needs of your people are great, but their knowledge is brief. Let it be your will, O LORD, our God, that you give to each person according to his needs and to each body according to its lack. Blessed is the one who hears prayer."[29]

While it is tempting to see the *Our Father* in these terms, there are important differences between it and these examples. There is no indication that *Our Father* is to be prayed only in times of distress or when traveling. Also, each of these prayers follows a set pattern: a vague petition that God fulfill Israel's requests followed by the conclusion, "Blessed is the one who hears prayer." This pattern does not match Yeshua's prayer.

The true purpose of *Our Father* may be revealed by a contextual clue. In Luke 11:1 the disciples ask Yeshua, "Teach us to pray, as John taught his disciples." This request is odd. Did the disciples not know how to pray, having been immersed in Jewish tradition since birth? Furthermore, if they were aware of the request of John's disciples, then why couldn't they have accepted John's answer to the question?

The Mishnah teaches that "if one makes his prayer 'fixed,' then it is not a true supplication."[30] The rabbis of the Gemara discuss what the sages of the Mishnah meant by "fixed" (since it certainly does not exclude all prewritten prayer). They also posit solutions as to how one should avoid a fixed prayer. One idea that the Gemara provides is to use an expressive voice when praying. Other rabbis solved this by appending a personal touch to the end of the *Amidah*, which they taught their disciples. Some of these prayers are recorded in the Talmud.[31] Here is an example of the personal prayer of Rabbi Elazar:

> Let it be your will, O LORD our God, that you let love,
> brotherhood, peace, and companionship take residence
> in our lives. Let our boundaries expand with disciples. Let
> us successfully finish with a future and hope, and make a
> place for us in the Garden of Eden. Affirm us with a good
> friend and a good inclination in your world. Let us rise
> each morning and find that the yearning in our heart is
> to fear your name. Let our spiritual needs come before
> you for the good.

The concept of the personal petition added to the *Amidah*
accords with the emphasis that Yeshua placed on heartfelt devotion during prayer. It fits the model of a prayer that is composed
by individual rabbis for use by their disciples. Furthermore, the
prayer that Yeshua taught seems to fit very well in this category,
since is it similar to the post-*Amidah* petitions both in length and
content. Rav Safra's prayer was that God would "establish peace in
the heavenly retinue and in the earthly retinue." Rava asked God
to help him "sin no more" and begged that God compassionately
purify him of those sins he had already committed. Both Rebbi and
Mar ben Ravina petitioned God to deliver them from anything evil.

Was *Our Father* intended as a post-*Amidah* petition? If so, it
would explain why the *Didache* instructs disciples to recite this
prayer three times a day—in keeping with the three daily recitations of the *Amidah*.

Further strengthening this position, Luke 11:1 specifically notes
that his disciples asked about this prayer *when Yeshua finished
praying*—which implies when he finished reciting the *Amidah*.

The *Amidah* constitutes the culmination of the prayer service.
Upon reaching this prayer, one should consider himself or herself
as standing before the very throne of God. It is the perfect opportunity to offer the petitions that are dearest to us; as disciples of
Yeshua, these desires are encapsulated in *Our Father*.

"OUR FATHER WHO IS IN HEAVEN"

God is called by many titles in Scripture and in other Jewish literature. The title by which one addresses God typically reflects
the attribute to which one wishes to draw attention.

The title "Father" for God is common throughout the Hebrew Scriptures and in Jewish prayer. This title draws attention to God's attribute of compassion. Psalm 103:13 teaches, "As a father shows compassion to his children, so the LORD shows compassion to those who fear him." Allusions to this verse appear in the *Slichot* prayers of repentance in the Siddur.

The phrase "our Father who is in heaven" in Hebrew is *avinu shebashamayim*. This is a common title for God in Judaism. For example, the sages of the Mishnah describe perilous times before the coming of the Messiah and conclude, "Upon whom can we rely? On our Father, who is in heaven."[32] The address "our Father who is in heaven" also introduces the *Prayer for the Welfare of the State of Israel*, a fairly new prayer found in Siddurim that reflect a Modern Orthodox or Religious Zionist tradition.

Luke's version is simply addressed to "Father" (which may reflect the Aramaic title *Abba*).

But the difference between Luke's version and Matthew's is not as dramatic as it might seem. The "our" in "our Father" primarily serves as a vocative marker. In other words, it feels more natural in Hebrew to address God as "our Father" rather than simply "Father." In English something similar occurs with the word "my" in phrases like "my dear" or "my lord."

The clause "who is in heaven" serves to distinguish God from an earthly father. An anecdote in the Talmud[33] tells of a pious man named Chanan HaNechba who was known for having his prayers for rain answered. The rabbis would send him schoolchildren, who would beg, "Abba, Abba, give us rain!" He would pray, "Act for the sake of these children who do not perceive the difference between the Abba that gives rain and the Abba that does not give rain" (or according to some manuscripts, "between Chanan and their Father who is in heaven").

According to scholar Brad H. Young, Luke may have intentionally omitted the phrase "who is in heaven" for the sake of his audience, who may have taken this phrase too literally, confusing HaShem's characteristics with those of—in complete contrast—Greek gods.

The personal name of God is spelled with four consonants that roughly correspond to the letters *Y*, *H*, *V*, and *H*. Observant Jews hallow this name of God by refraining from attempting to pronounce it the way it is spelled, instead employing evasive synonyms such as "Lord" and "Father." Yeshua upheld this tradition, teaching his disciples to set God's name apart as holy by addressing him as "Father."

"LET YOUR NAME BE SANCTIFIED"

This phrase is strongly reminiscent of an ancient prayer called the *Kaddish*. The *Kaddish* is recited many times in each prayer service as a transition between one section of prayer and another. It begins with the line, "Let his name be magnified and sanctified in the world that he created as he willed."

One of the blessings of the *Amidah* declares the holiness of God's name:

> You are holy, and your name is holy, and holy ones praise
> you every day—Selah. Blessed are you, O LORD, the holy
> God.

On a basic level, to be sanctified means to be made or treated as holy. However, the sanctification of God's name (Kiddush HaShem) is a developed concept in Jewish thought. Sanctification of God's name can refer to either of two things: bringing glory to God and his reputation in the eyes of others or losing one's life as a martyr for the sake of God's name.

By expressing in a passive voice that God's name should be sanctified, we leave out the agent of the sanctification. Who is it that should sanctify God's name? Are we asking that humans sanctify God's name or that God sanctify it himself?

In the phrase "magnified and sanctified," the *Kaddish* alludes to a passage in Ezekiel that describes the aftermath of the apocalyptic war of Gog and Magog:

> So I will show my greatness [*vehitgaddilti*, וְהִתְגַּדִּלְתִּי] and
> my holiness [*vehitkaddishti*, וְהִתְקַדִּשְׁתִּי] and make myself
> known in the eyes of many nations. Then they will know
> that I am the LORD. (Ezekiel 38:23)

Ezekiel and the *Kaddish* use not a purely passive grammatical form but a reflexive one. It is likely that Yeshua also used a reflexive form in his prayer, as shown in nearly all Hebrew translations of *Our Father*. This means that rather than the simple "may your name be sanctified," the phrase carries the sense of "let your name reveal its holiness." In such usage God is shown to be the agent of his name's sanctification.

Yeshua's prayer also alludes to God's Messianic promise through Ezekiel to vindicate his name that is profaned among the nations in exile:

> I will vindicate the holiness of [literally: "sanctify"] my great name, which has been profaned among the nations, and which you have profaned among them. And the nations will know that I am the LORD, declares the Lord GOD, when through you I vindicate my holiness [literally: "am sanctified"] before their eyes. (Ezekiel 36:23)

On this verse Rashi asks, "What is the sanctification spoken of here?" He explains that it is the return from exile prophesied in the following verse:

> I will take you from the nations and gather you from all the countries and bring you into your own land. (Ezekiel 36:24)

Thus, when we pray that God's name be sanctified, we are asking God to fulfill his promise to end the exile and bring redemption.

"LET YOUR KINGDOM COME"

Again, *Our Father* bears similarity to the *Kaddish*, which asks, "May he inaugurate his kingdom." This refers to the Messianic Era, when the sovereignty of God will be fully revealed on earth.

Surely God reigns as King even now; the writers of the Targums were sensitive to that fact when translating verses that appear to place God's rule solely in the future. The Targums went to great lengths to insist that God's kingship is present but needs only to be revealed:

Direct Translation of Hebrew	Translation of Targum Yonatan
"The LORD will be king over all the earth." (Zechariah 14:9)	The kingship of the LORD will be revealed over all inhabitants of the earth.
"The kingdom shall be the LORD's." (Obadiah 21)	The kingship of the LORD will soon be revealed over all the inhabitants of the earth, and the kingship of the LORD will endure forever and ever.

Yeshua's plea that God's kingdom come should be understood the same way: let God's kingdom, which is currently hidden, be revealed to all the inhabitants on earth. This will be the case in the Messianic Era.

The message of the coming kingdom was central to Yeshua's teachings; it was the core of the "good news" that he proclaimed: "Repent, for the kingdom of heaven is at hand" (Matthew 4:17).

With these opening lines of *Our Father*, an interesting pattern occurs. Jewish law requires that a formal blessing contain references both to the name of God and to his kingship (*shem umalchut*).[34] Even though *Our Father* is not a blessing in this sense, it contains both of these elements.

The first two lines of *Our Father* also bear notable similarity to a line from the prayer *Baruch HaShem Le'olam* ("Blessed Is the LORD Forever"), recited in the weekday *ma'ariv* service between the *Shma* and the *Amidah*. One line from this prayer reads, "Our God who is in heaven, unify your name; continually uphold your kingdom, and reign over us forever and ever." However, although both *Our Father* and *Baruch HaShem Le'olam* look forward to the kingdom of God, the similarity in wording is most likely coincidental. *Baruch HaShem Le'olam* was added to the *ma'ariv* service during the Middle Ages.

"LET YOUR WILL BE DONE"

The request "let your will be done" has provocative implications. Why would God's will not be done in the first place? And who are we to give him permission to do what he wants?

Pirkei Avot is a famous collection of ancient rabbinic wisdom. Rabban Gamliel III, who lived in the third century, offered this advice:

> Carry out [God's] will as your will, in order that he will carry out your will as his will. Nullify your own will on account of his will, in order that he will nullify the will of others on account of your will.[35]

Accordingly, the statement "let your will be done" is in one sense not a petition but an expression of devotion: "I submit myself to your will." Similarly, Yeshua said in great anguish regarding his execution, "Father, if you are willing, remove this cup from me. Nevertheless, not my will, but yours, be done" (Luke 22:42). As David proclaimed, "I delight to do your will, O my God; your law is within my heart" (Psalm 40:9[8]).

Nonetheless, both the words of Yeshua and those of Rabban Gamliel imply that (from a human vantage point) God's will can be changed or suppressed and that it is not always being carried out on earth.

The prayer of second-century Rabbi Elazar ben Shammua provides a notable parallel to the phrase "let your will be done" but with important differences. As noted in the introduction to this section, Rabbi Elazar offered this prayer when traveling in a dangerous situation:

> Do your will in heaven, give relief to those who fear you on earth, and do what is good in your sight. Blessed is the one who hears prayer.[36]

Rabbi Elazar's petition is, "Do your will in heaven." Rashi explains that in heaven there is no sin, and thus God's will is for the benefit of all who are there. But on earth below our situation is unfortunately much different. Rabbi Elazar's request could be elucidated, "Do your will freely in heaven, where all are in good standing; but do not do so on earth, where we are culpable for sin. Rather, give relief to those who fear you on earth." This reflects the concept that when God executes his will, each person is repaid according to his deeds (compare Psalm 62:12; Job 34:11; Matthew

16:27; Revelation 22:12). God suppresses this will on earth out of his mercy on us who fall short of his demands.

In contrast, Yeshua's petition is that God's will be done on earth just as it is in heaven. At face value this request seems to contradict that of Rabbi Elazar. However, Rabbi Elazar's request relates to our current personal situation here and now. Yeshua's request is far broader in scope, asking not just for mercy upon the sinful but the elimination of sin itself with the advent of the Messianic Kingdom.

"As in Heaven, So on Earth"

Heaven and earth are frequently contrasted in Jewish writings. Heaven (sometimes called "above") is the place where God's kingship is manifest; on earth ("below") his kingship is obscured. The goal of redemption is to cause the lower world to reflect the upper world.

In Jewish interpretation, when Moses ascended Mount Sinai, he was not simply shown a diagram of the Tabernacle but was given a tour of the actual heavenly abode of God. He was instructed to make a replica of the supernal Sanctuary in the midst of Israel. Likewise, Revelation 21 offers a glimpse of the heavenly Jerusalem descending to earth.

The phrase "as in heaven, so on earth" does not apply only to the expression "let your will be done" but to all three of the preceding petitions. Rabbi Yechiel Lichtenstein, Messianic Jewish luminary from the nineteenth century, wrote,

> Yeshua's expression, "As in heaven, so on earth," relates to each of his phrases: "Let your name be sanctified," "let your kingdom come," and "let your will be done." As in heaven—where your name is sanctified, where the kingdom of God is, and where his will is done among "his ministers, who do his will" (Psalm 103:21)—so on earth, let your name be sanctified, and let your kingdom come, and let your will be done.

Not only does Rabbi Lichtenstein's interpretation make sense in light of Jewish thought, it also accords with the interpretation presented in the *Roman Catechism of the Council of Trent* (1566).

The *Kedushah* section of the *Amidah* depicts the heavenly worship service. Borrowing from Isaiah 6, the Siddur describes the angels surrounding the throne and declaring the holiness of God constantly, crying, "Holy, holy, holy." The *Kedushah* opens with the words, "We will sanctify your name in the world as it is sanctified in the highest heights." In other words, "As in heaven, so on earth."

"BREAD OF TOMORROW"

As uncommon as the translation "bread of tomorrow" is, there is strong and widespread scholarly support for it. The primary reason that the translation "daily bread" is so pervasive today is because of the momentum of Christian liturgical tradition in the use of the phrase.

Most commentators see the petition typically translated "give us this day our daily bread" as a humble request for simple sustenance. The Hebrew word for "bread," *lechem* (לֶחֶם), is often used to represent all food. For example, Psalm 136:25 reads that God "gives food [*lechem*] to all flesh, for his steadfast love endures forever." Thus, this petition can be understood to mean, "Provide us with each day's sustenance."

However, this passage contains a mystery that calls into question this seemingly simple interpretation. The Greek word that translators traditionally render as "daily" is *epiousios* (ἐπιούσιος). This word appears in Matthew, Luke, and the *Didache* in their quotations of the Master's prayer but nowhere else in Greek literature. It is not the normal way to say "daily" in Greek. Origen, a third-century Christian scholar and theologian, suggested that the writers of the Gospels invented the Greek word themselves.

Some scholars suggest that we should interpret *epiousios* as a combination of the Greek preposition *epi* (ἐπι) and the verb *einai* (εἶναι), which means "to be." This results in something like "for the existing [day]," that is, "daily." Others see it as a combination of *epi* and the word *ousia* (οὐσία), which means "being, existence." This makes it "[required] for existence," that is, "needful."

Franz Delitzsch favored "needful" and saw it as an allusion to Proverbs 30:8: "Feed me with the food that is my portion" (NASB). His translation of Matthew 6:11 follows the Hebrew of this verse.

If Matthew 6:11 were an allusion to Proverbs 30:8, we would expect the Greek versions of these two verses to match; in most cases New Testament quotations from the Hebrew Scriptures are similar to the Greek of the Septuagint. But the Greek wording of the Septuagint in this verse of Proverbs is nothing like the Greek text of Matthew. This casts doubt on the connection between the two verses.

Both the "daily" and "needful" interpretations also have a grammatical problem. If the words for "daily" or "needful" were meant, then according to Greek grammatical rules, we should expect the first *iota* (or letter *i* when transcribed in English) not to be present in the resulting word. It should be *epousios*, not *epiousios*.

For this reason some scholars say that the word is a combination of *epi* and *ienai* (ἰέναι), which means "to go" or "to come." The combined word means "coming after," and it doesn't have the spelling problem of the other theories. A similarly formed word appears in Proverbs 3:28 and 27:1 as *epiousa* (ἐπιοῦσα), and it means "the next day," that is, "tomorrow." By this interpretation the verse could be understood, "Give us today our *tomorrowly* bread." ("Tomorrowly" isn't a real word, but neither is *epiousios*.) In this case the words "today" and "tomorrow[ly]" complement each other nicely.

Another piece of evidence provides strong support for the "tomorrowly" interpretation. Jerome, a Christian priest, theologian, and historian of the fourth century, is well known for translating the Bible into Latin. He also wrote commentaries on much of Scripture. One of the sources that he occasionally referred to was a document called the Gospel of the Hebrews. This was a collection of sayings and stories about the Master used by the Jewish disciples of Yeshua, and it was written in the Hebrew language. Many of the church fathers mentioned and quoted from this document (and others like it), but it is no longer extant today.

Jerome himself interpreted *epiousios* as "over-being," which he translated into Latin as *supersubstantialem* (as in "super-substantial"). But in his commentary on Matthew 6:11, he noted,

> In the Gospel which is called "according to the Hebrews," I have found instead of "supersubstantial" bread, *maar*, which means "tomorrow's." Thus the sense is: "give us today our" tomorrow's, that is, future, "bread."[37]

The Hebrew word meaning "tomorrow" that Jerome noted was *machar* (מָחָר). This means that according to the tradition of the ancient Jewish disciples of Yeshua, the prayer said, "Give us today our bread of tomorrow." Scholar Raymond E. Brown notes that this reading is also supported by the ancient Coptic versions of the New Testament.

Whether we are praying for "daily bread" or for "bread of tomorrow," it might seem to be the same idea in both cases: "Provide for our immediate need." However, this interpretation still has problems.

Later on in this very chapter of Matthew, Yeshua advises us not to worry about what we will eat or drink. He teaches, "Your heavenly Father knows that you need them all" (Matthew 6:32). He instructs us not to be anxious about tomorrow but rather to "seek first the kingdom of God and his righteousness, and all these will be added to [us]" (Matthew 6:33). Rabbi Eliezer ben Hyrcanus, an important sage who lived during the time of the apostles, even said, "Whoever has bread in his basket and asks, 'What will I eat tomorrow?' is among those of little faith."[38] Considering these statements, it seems odd that Yeshua would instruct us to petition God to meet our basic needs, especially tomorrow's basic needs.

Granted, this could simply be understood as a faithful expression of trust in God as our sole provider and a recognition that when we do receive our daily bread, it comes from him. However, the beginning of *Our Father* is focused broadly on the redemption and the revelation of God. A transition from this universal kingdom focus to our personal earthly needs would be jarring; it seems out of place.

It might seem that Yeshua referred to basic needs when he instructed, "Ask, and it will be given to you" (Matthew 7:7) and then asked, "Which one of you, if his son asks him for bread, will give him a stone?" (Matthew 7:9). However, the "good gifts" spoken of here also appear to be kingdom-focused and not basic necessities. Luke's version concludes, "How much more will the heavenly Father give *the Holy Spirit* to those who ask him!" (Luke 11:13, emphasis added).

Perhaps "bread of tomorrow" has a deeper implication. Jerome referred to this reading in his Gospel of the Hebrews again in his commentary on the verse "he who gives food [*lechem*] to all flesh" (Psalm 136:25 [135:25 in the Septuagint]):

> The Hebrew Gospel according to Matthew reads: "Give us this day tomorrow's bread," in other words, the Bread that You will give us in Your kingdom, give us this day.[39]

Some scholars, including Raymond Brown and Joachim Jeremias, also see this petition as relating to the Messianic Kingdom.

The kingdom is frequently described in terms of a great banquet. Someone reclining at a meal with Yeshua once reacted to his teachings by exclaiming, "Blessed is everyone who will eat bread in the kingdom of God!" (Luke 14:15). In the book of Revelation Yeshua promises that "to the one who conquers [he] will give some of the hidden manna" (Revelation 2:17).

Thus, by asking for the "tomorrowly bread" to come to us today, we are asking for the substance of the Messianic Era to be present in our daily lives even as we strive in the current age. We also express hope that today is the day that we will finally feast at the lavish banquet of the Messianic Kingdom.

"PARDON OUR DEBTS"

In Luke's version we ask God to pardon our *sins*, but Matthew refers to these as *debts*. Many scholars have noted the Semitic flavor of Matthew's wording. Since Luke was writing for a less Jewish-literate audience, he opted for a less idiomatic term. Matthew reflects the original language more directly.

Chovah (חוֹבָה) is a Hebrew and Aramaic word that means both "a sin" and "a debt." It also frequently denotes "an obligation." For example, if a person is required to fulfill a certain commandment, then it can be called a *chovah*.

If a person wrongs his fellow, such as by causing damage to his property, he is liable to pay for the property to be restored. In this case his liability is his *chovah*.

But even if a person commits a sin against God, he may become liable to a penalty in this world or in the afterlife. For such a person, his penalty is the *chovah*—a payment that he is obligated to make.

Thus, in the Jewish economy of sin and restitution, the guilt caused by sin is equated to a debt, so both sin against man and against God can be called a *chovah*. The claimant of a debt, whether God or man, has every right either to demand payment or to pardon the debt, canceling what is owed.

In Jewish thought there is a clear difference between forgiveness and pardon. Forgiveness (*slichah*, סְלִיחָה) is the relinquishing of anger resulting from an offense. One who has forgiven another no longer harbors bitter feelings. Pardon (*mechilah*, מְחִילָה) is cancellation of the debt that is owed as a result of the offense.

For example, if Jerry throws a baseball through Frank's window, Frank might become very angry. If Frank *forgives* Jerry, he sets aside his feelings of anger about the broken window. But although there are no hard feelings, Jerry is still responsible to pay for repairs. It is only once Frank *pardons* Jerry's debt that he is no longer required to pay.

The petition "pardon our debts" is similar to the sixth blessing of the *Amidah*:

> Forgive us, our Father, for we have sinned. Pardon us, our King, for we have transgressed. For you pardon and forgive.

Just as the *Amidah* looks forward to the ultimate redemption with this plea, *Our Father* also has the kingdom in view. The petition "pardon our debts" begins with a conspicuous "and," tying this petition to the previous one. It brings the immediacy of "give us *today*" into the context.

Yeshua came proclaiming that the Messianic Era was attainable. He also warned that the sins of the generation that heard him would lead to the destruction of the Temple and to exile. According to both Jewish tradition and the teachings of Yeshua, the primary transgression at fault was enmity and discord among the Jewish people.

Third-century Rabbi Yochanan bar Nafcha related an anecdote the events of which he claims led to the destruction of Jerusalem. In this story the enmity between two men caused one to humiliate the other in the presence of the rabbis, who did nothing to intervene. The shamed individual went to the Roman emperor to seek revenge.[40]

The core of Yeshua's message was "Love your neighbor as yourself" (Leviticus 19:18), which is the antidote to hatred. Yeshua warned that if one was offering a sacrifice and remembered that his fellow harbored an offense against him, he should make reconciliation a priority even over the sacrifice (Matthew 5:23–24). This is because strife between brothers would lead to the Temple's destruction; without reconciliation, there would be no venue for sacrifices. Yeshua continued,

> Come to terms quickly with your accuser while you are going with him to court, lest your accuser hand you over to the judge, and the judge to the guard, and you be put in prison. Truly, I say to you, you will never get out until you have paid the last penny. (Matthew 5:25–26)

"Prison" is a metaphor for exile. The guilt incurred by sin is thus likened to a monetary debt.

In the verses that follow, Yeshua teaches that an individual who is wronged should not rely on the Torah's principle of "an eye for an eye" (Matthew 5:38). In other words, one should not demand payback from those who wronged him, even though it is within his rights. After all, "with the measure [we] use it will be measured to [us]" (Matthew 7:2). If a person demands strict justice against those who wrong him, God will likewise demand strict justice against him.

Rabbi Yochanan bar Nafcha proposed that the unwillingness of people to waive their legal rights contributed to the destruction of Jerusalem.[41] Since the inhabitants of Jerusalem were quick to demand that others be punished for their wrongs, so God decreed strict punishment against them.

One of the sages had a creative interpretation of Micah 7:18, describing God as "pardoning iniquity and passing over transgression." Rabba read the Hebrew to mean that God "pardons iniquity of one who passes over transgression." He explained, "If one passes over his right to exact punishment [from whose who wronged him], God will pass over all his transgressions."[42]

According to Jewish tradition, one must seek forgiveness from others prior to Yom Kippur.[43] This is because one cannot simply ask

God to forgive a sin that was committed against another person. The person who was wronged deserves the right to forgive the sin.

But when one does not forgive and pardon another, not only is the sin itself hanging unresolved, but God's attribute of justice is more intensely focused on the one who is wronged. A frequently expressed tenet of Judaism is that "all Israel are responsible for one another."[44] As such, everyone suffers as a result of strife.

Only when we pardon the debts that others owe us will God pardon the debts that we owe him. When God has truly cleared us of our debts, the redemption will begin. Like the bread of tomorrow, we desire such pardon today.

"Do Not Let Us Be Overcome by Trials"

The conventional translation "lead us not into temptation" is problematic. By asking God not to lead us into temptation, it implies that sometimes he does. But James says,

> Let no one say when he is tempted, "I am being tempted by God," for God cannot be tempted with evil, and he himself tempts no one. But each person is tempted when he is lured and enticed by his own desire. (James 1:13–14)

But both the Greek word for "temptation," *peirasmos* (πειρασμός), and its equivalent in Hebrew, *nissayon* (נִסָּיוֹן), mean "testing" or "trial."

The difference between temptation and testing is the desired outcome on the part of the one controlling the circumstances. If one desires to see his subject fail, then it is a temptation. If he wants to prove his subject worthy, then it is a test.

Nissayon is a common way to describe difficult circumstances. But rather than simply "troubles" or "suffering," the word *nissayon* implies that there is a purpose to our hardship.

In Jewish thought testing is an important part of life. It benefits the person being tested because by passing tests, one gains merit. According to Jewish tradition, Abraham was tested ten times, including when he was told to leave his home and family (Genesis 12) and when he bound Isaac (Genesis 22). These tests served to show the great depth of Abraham's love for God.[45] In Jewish tradition the merit of Abraham as a result of his trials has served to support and benefit the Jewish people.

An illustration might demonstrate how testing produces merit. Suppose there was a soldier who fought bravely in a war. He was not extraordinarily strong or well trained, but as a result of his determination and effort, he succeeded against his enemy. When the king came to present the soldier his award of valor, a second warrior who was twice the size of the first and fully trained demanded the same award, even though he had not spent even one day on the battlefield. When the king objected that it would not be fair, the second warrior answered, "If he was able to achieve what he did being weak and untrained, then surely I who am far more capable would have accomplished the same." The warrior, of course, was a fool, because it is the experience, suffering, and real accomplishment on the part of the individual that merits reward rather than his or her intrinsic greatness.

Thus, testing is to our great advantage. James said, "Count it all joy, my brothers, when you meet trials of various kinds" (James 1:2), indicating that the end result of testing is our perfection and completion.

All humans undergo tests. If testing is beneficial to us, why then should we pray not to be tested?

Although such testing is to our benefit if we succeed, the early rabbis advised that one should not purposely seek to be tested by God.[46] Furthermore, in *Our Father* we do not ask, "Do not test us," but, "Do not lead us *into* testing." The meaning of this can be clarified with numerous parallels in Jewish prayer.

One page of the Talmud lists two prayers that one should offer, one in the morning and one in the evening, both of which have made it into the daily Siddur.[47] The evening prayer includes the lines:

> Do not let me be overcome by sin or overcome by iniquity or overcome by trials or overcome by contempt.
> … Rescue me from harmful circumstances and from harmful illnesses.

The morning prayer asks,

Do not let me be overcome by sin or overcome by iniquity or overcome by trials or overcome by contempt. … Distance me from a harmful person or from a harmful friend.

In these prayers a rigid word-for-word translation of the phrase "do not let me overcome by" is "lead me not into the hand of." The word for hand, *yad* (יָד), is included in many idioms, and in contexts like this it can mean "influence," "power," "control," or "care."

In both prayers we ask God not to lead us into the *influence* of trials; in other words, though trials come, let us not succumb to them. This is probably the same wording that Yeshua would have used in his prayer.

Both prayers contrast being led to bad influences with being rescued (or distanced) from what is harmful. The word for "harmful" is *ra* (רַע), which is often translated "evil." In Jewish thought the essence of evil is destructiveness, which is why an illness (which is not in any sense immoral) can be called *ra*.

The post-*Amidah* prayer of Rabbi Yehudah HaNasi, who compiled the Mishnah, carries a similar theme of deliverance from *ra*:

Let it be your will, O LORD, my God and God of my fathers, that you rescue me today and every day from those who are insolent and from the trait of insolence, from a harmful individual, from a harmful incident, from a harmful friend, from a harmful neighbor, from the destructive adversary, from harsh judgments or harsh legal opponents, whether they are covenant members or not covenant members.[48]

This prayer was ultimately incorporated into the traditional daily prayers.

Rabbi Chiya bar Ashi had the habit of praying, "May the Compassionate One rescue us from the evil inclination."[49] By this he meant, "Help me not give in to the temptation to sin."

"RESCUE US FROM WHAT IS EVIL"

The final clause of *Our Father* says, "Rescue us from what is evil." Based on this context, we can better understand what Yeshua meant in his prayer.

In the prayers listed above, evil (*ra*) represents anything harmful that may befall us, especially our own evil inclination. The evil inclination (*yetzer ha-ra*, יֵצֶר הָרַע) is our animalistic impulse that causes us to sin. The New Testament sometimes expresses that these tendencies relate to our "flesh."

The two lines "do not let us be overcome by trials" and "but rescue us from what is evil" form a common type of Hebrew parallelism. The structure strongly suggests that the "evil" that we are to be rescued from is our own impulse that can lead us to fail in the face of testing. Alternatively, it could be the harmful result of failing such a test.

Both the Greek phrase (*ho poneros*, ὁ πονηρὸς) and its Hebrew equivalent (*ha-ra*, הָרַע) could be translated "the evil one." But in Jewish thought there is a close connection between Satan and the evil inclination within ourselves in that both entice us to sin.

This petition is eschatological (end-times related) in nature as well. In his commentary on the Gospel of Matthew, Levertoff wrote,

> "Temptation" probably means the days of trial which will accompany the coming of the kingdom—days of difficulty and suffering for the followers of the Lord. We are to pray for deliverance from these evils and for strength to withstand them. [50]

Yeshua taught that along with the revelation of the kingdom, there would be difficult times. Some of those came to pass during the Jewish-Roman wars, but there remain some "birth pangs" that will accompany the Messiah's return. Yeshua taught us that not everyone will endure these trials:

> Many will fall away and betray one another and hate one another. And many false prophets will arise and lead many astray. And because lawlessness will be increased, the love of many will grow cold. But the one who endures to the end will be saved. (Matthew 24:10–14)

Rabbinic literature also describes the troubles that will accompany the arrival of Messiah. The end of tractate *Sotah* in the Mishnah describes the corruption of this generation and says that even scholars and leaders will turn astray.

The *Didache* also warns about the future tribulations:

> The entire human race will enter the trial by fire, and many will be caused to stumble and will perish, but those who endure in their faithfulness will be saved by the very one who is cursed.[51]

The world is becoming darker with each passing generation. It is now more important than ever that we seek strength from our Father in heaven.

"YOURS IS THE KINGDOM AND THE POWER AND THE MAJESTY"

The final line of *Our Father* is a doxology, a common feature in ancient Jewish prayer. It is not in the oldest manuscripts of Matthew, and modern scholars agree that it was not a part of the original prayer. It is included in the *Didache*, and it is likely that it was appended to *Our Father* very early for liturgical use among the believers.

A doxology is a brief liturgical form. Doxologies typically begin with an ascription of praise to God, followed by any of various expressions meaning "forever" and the word "amen." They are often used to conclude a section of a liturgical service.

Doxologies appear in several places in both the Hebrew Scriptures and in the New Testament. For example, Psalm 89 concludes with the line, "Blessed be the LORD forever! Amen and Amen." Similarly, Psalm 72:19 says, "Blessed be his glorious name forever; may the whole earth be filled with his glory! Amen and Amen!" In Revelation 7:12, the angels are depicted worshiping God with the words, "Amen! Blessing and glory and wisdom and thanksgiving and honor and power and might be to our God forever and ever! Amen."

The doxology of *Our Father* seems to be inspired by David's blessing:

> Yours, O LORD, is the greatness and the power and the glory and the victory and the majesty, for all that is in the heavens and in the earth is yours. Yours is the king-

dom, O LORD, and you are exalted as head above all.
(1 Chronicles 29:11)

In Jewish prayer the *Kaddish* functions as a doxology. Another doxology in Jewish liturgy is the prayer *Yishtabach*, which includes these lines:

> For you, O LORD, our God and God of our fathers, are worthy to receive songs and acclamation, praise and music, strength and dominion, everlastingness, greatness and power, praise and majesty, holiness and kingship, blessings and thanks from now to eternity.

The phrase "yours is the kingdom" also appears in the prayer *Aleinu*:

> They will all accept the yoke of your kingdom, and you will reign over them soon, forever and ever. For yours is the kingdom, and forever and ever you will reign with glory. As it is written in your Torah: "The LORD will reign forever and ever!"

Even though the *Our Father* did not include the doxological ending at first, it is appropriate for us to include it when we pray, since it reflects the liturgical tradition of a very early generation of disciples.

PRAYER FOR THE RESTORATION OF ZION

O Lord, in accordance with all your acts of righteousness, let your anger and wrath turn away from your city Jerusalem, your holy mountain. Our Father, our King, lift a banner to the peoples to return Israel to its pasture. Gather us together from the four corners of the earth to our land, and plant us within its borders on the mountain of our inheritance. Bring us to Zion, your city, with singing and to Jerusalem, your holy city, with eternal joy. Build it in your compassion, and let it remain perched and inhabited in its place. Establish your holy Temple in it, and gladden us in your House of Prayer. Return your Dwelling Presence to Zion, your city, and send us Yeshua our Messiah a second time. Let him reign upon the throne of David in Jerusalem, your holy city. Lift up the horn of the salvations of your people Israel in the house of David your servant—salvation from our enemies and from the hand of all who hate us, just as you have spoken through your prophets. O Lord, hear! O Lord, forgive! O Lord, listen and act! Do not delay, for your own sake, our God, for your name is called upon your city and upon your people. Hurry, LORD, to help us! Ransom your people Israel from all its iniquities and from all its troubles, for the time to be gracious has come, for the appointed time has come. Amen.

An introduction to the basics of Messianic Jewish prayer would be incomplete if it did not include some representation of the work of the Messianic Jewish pioneers of the last two centuries.

The Legacy of Messianic Judaism

Messianic Judaism has a long and fascinating heritage, going back to the disciples of Yeshua, who practiced Judaism their entire lives. Modern Messianic Judaism was birthed in the nineteenth century. At that time several prominent, well-educated Jewish people came to the realization that Yeshua of Nazareth was the redeemer of Israel. They also felt that this fact should not change who they were as Jews devoted to the Torah and to their people.

The luminaries of that generation faced an uphill battle, and yet they paved the way for the Messianic Jewish community that exists today. Some of these men were adept writers and poets; their works serve as a blessing and inspiration to us.

Rabbi Yechiel Tzvi Lichtenstein

Rabbi Yechiel Tzvi Lichtenstein was born and raised in a Chasidic family in Moldavia in 1831. He was fully educated as a rebbe in the thriving Chasidic community of Iaşi, Romania, but after functioning as a rebbe for some time, he resigned because he did not feel comfortable with the homage paid to him. Later he and some friends read a copy of the New Testament and were drawn to the mystical concepts in the Gospel of John.

As a believer in Yeshua, Rabbi Lichtenstein remained firmly committed to Judaism; he and his friends initially attempted to integrate as a contingent of disciples of Yeshua within the Jewish community. It did not go as he planned; he was excommunicated, and his friends gave in to the pressure to renounce Yeshua.

Rabbi Lichtenstein eventually got in touch with other Jewish believers, wrote several books, including a commentary on the New Testament, and assisted Franz Delitzsch with his Hebrew translation.

The Restoration of Zion

Rabbi Lichtenstein's "Prayer for the Restoration of Zion" appears in a Messianic Jewish Hebrew periodical called *Edut LeYisrael*. This periodical was edited by Theophilus Lucky and published both in the United States and in Eastern Europe. It was one of the first Hebrew periodicals published in America.

This prayer was printed in the context of an article describing Lucky's experience of frustration as a Messianic Jew. Lucky and his fellow Jewish believers prayed constantly for Jerusalem's restoration and longed for the Jewish people to be returned to their homeland. In contrast, he noticed an alarming number of Jewish people in his country who did not seem to care about Jerusalem. They did not even fast and attend the synagogue on the traditional fast day of the ninth of Av. And despite their own lack of Jewish observance alongside his firm commitment to Torah and Jewish tradition, those were the people who would accuse him of being an apostate for his faith in Yeshua.

Lucky introduced Lichtenstein's prayer as an example of the heart for the restoration of Jerusalem that was prevalent among Messianic Jews. He introduced the prayer by saying,

> We mention Jerusalem in all of our prayers. And anyone who reads the prayer of Yechiel Even-Tzohar the Chasid with any heart will weep with us over the fate of Jerusalem and pray as we do.

Rabbi Lichtenstein's prayer is a tapestry of numerous sources, including references from the Hebrew Scriptures, the New Testament, and a variety of passages from every corner of the Siddur. Rabbi Lichtenstein was clearly well acquainted with all of them.

The most striking aspect of Rabbi Lichtenstein's prayer is its thoroughly Jewish perspective. His hope was in the literal regathering of the Jewish people, the restoration of the physical city of Jerusalem, and the rebuilding of the Temple as an actual house of prayer. These sentiments were largely unwelcome in mainstream Christianity, especially in his time.

PART 3

THE TEXT
OF THE PRAYERS

THE PRAYERS AND BLESSINGS

H ere we have provided the basic text of some of the core prayers of the Jewish prayer service. Please note that they have been simplified in order to aid beginners and reduce the learning curve. A complete traditional prayer service is far more extensive, and it includes special readings at times such as holidays or the new moon (Rosh Chodesh). To see the complete prayer service, consult a Siddur.

Here is a suggested schedule that you could follow to embark on a pattern of daily prayer:

	Morning	**Afternoon**	**Evening**
I Hereby Join	O	O	O
Declaration of Intent for Messianic Gentiles*	Y	Y	Y
Shma	Y	N	Y
Amidah	Y	Y	Y
Our Father	Y	Y	Y
Prayer for the Restoration of Zion	O	O	O

Y = Include, N = Exclude, O = Optional. *Omit if you are Jewish

This prayer is optional. Some disciples choose to include it once
a day or at the beginning of each prayer service.

I HEREBY JOIN MYSELF

to the Master, Yeshua the Messiah,
the righteous one, who is the bread of life
and the true light, the source of eternal
salvation for all those who hear him.

Like a branch that remains in a vine,
so may I remain in him, just as he also
remains in the Father and the Father in him,
in order that they may remain in us.

May the grace of the
Master, Yeshua the Messiah,
the love of God, and the fellowship
of the Holy Spirit abound to us.

This prayer is optional. Some disciples choose to include it once
a day or at the beginning of each prayer service.

הֲרֵינִי מְקַשֵּׁר עַצְמִי

בָּאָדוֹן, יֵשׁוּעַ הַמָּשִׁיחַ
הַצַּדִּיק, שֶׁהוּא לֶחֶם הַחַיִּים
וְהָאוֹר הָאֲמִתִּי, מַמְצִיא תְּשׁוּעַת
עוֹלָמִים לְכָל שֹׁמְעָיו.

כְּמוֹ שָׂרִיג שֶׁעוֹמֵד בַּגֶּפֶן,
כֵּן אֲנִי אֶעֱמוֹד בּוֹ, כַּאֲשֶׁר גַּם
הוּא עוֹמֵד בָּאָב וְהָאָב בּוֹ,
כְּדֵי שֶׁיַּעַמְדוּ בָנוּ.

חֵן הָאָדוֹן יֵשׁוּעַ
הַמָּשִׁיחַ וְאַהֲבַת הָאֱלֹהִים וְחֶבְרַת
רוּחַ הַקֹּדֶשׁ יֵרְבּוּ לָנוּ.

DECLARATION OF INTENT FOR MESSIANIC GENTILES

This prayer is recommended for Messianic Gentiles to recite before each prayer service.

WITH the permission of the heavenly assembly and with the permission of the earthly assembly, I hereby prepare my mouth to thank, praise, laud, petition, and serve my creator in the words of his people Israel. I cannot declare that Abraham fathered me, nor can I claim to be his offspring according to the flesh. For I am a branch from the stem of the children of Shem, Ham, and Japheth, like a wild olive branch grafted into a cultivated olive tree, in order to sprout forth and produce fruit in the name of all Israel.

FATHER IN HEAVEN, I will rejoice in you alone, for you have sanctified me and drawn me near to you, and you have made me a son of Abraham through your King Messiah. For the sake of our Master Yeshua, in his merit and virtues, may the sayings of my mouth and the meditation of my heart be joined to the prayers of all Israel, and may they be favorable before you, O LORD, my rock and my redeemer.

 SHMA

Recite this entire section twice a day: morning (shacharit) and evening (ma'ariv).
If you wear tzitziyot during shacharit, take all four in your left hand and hold them near your heart.

If a minyan is not present, say:

God is a faithful king.

DEUTERONOMY 6:4

COVER THE EYES. ALOUD, IN UNISON:

HEAR, O ISRAEL!
THE LORD IS OUR GOD; THE LORD IS ONE.

QUIETLY:

Blessed is the name of the glory of his kingdom forever and ever.

DECLARATION OF INTENT FOR MESSIANIC GENTILES

This prayer is recommended for Messianic Gentiles to recite before each prayer service.

בִּרְשׁוּת הַקָּהָל שֶׁל מַעְלָה וּבִרְשׁוּת הַקָּהָל שֶׁל מַטָּה, הֲרֵינִי מְזַמֵּן אֶת פִּי לְהוֹדוֹת וּלְהַלֵּל וּלְשַׁבֵּחַ וּלְהִתְחַנֵּן וְלַעֲבוֹד לִפְנֵי בּוֹרְאִי בְּדִבְרֵי עַמּוֹ יִשְׂרָאֵל. לֹא אוּכַל לְהַכְרִיז שֶׁאַבְרָהָם הוֹלִיד אוֹתִי, וְלֹא לִטְעוֹן לִהְיוֹת מִזַּרְעוֹ לְפִי הַבָּשָׂר. כִּי אֲנִי שָׂרִיג מִגֶּזַע בְּנֵי שֵׁם וְחָם וְיֶפֶת, כְּמוֹ זֵית הַיַּעַר, מוּרְכָּב עַל עֵץ זַיִת טוֹב, כְּדֵי לִצְמוֹחַ וְלַעֲשׂוֹת פְּרִי בְּשֵׁם כָּל יִשְׂרָאֵל.

אָבִי שֶׁבַּשָּׁמַיִם אֶשְׂמַח בְּךָ לְבַדְּךָ כִּי קִדַּשְׁתָּנִי וְקֵרַבְתָּנִי אֵלֶיךָ וְעֲשִׂיתָנִי בֶּן לְאַבְרָהָם עַל יְדֵי מֶלֶךְ מְשִׁיחֶךָ. לְמַעַן יֵשׁוּעַ רַבֵּנוּ, בִּזְכוּת וּזְכוּיוֹת שֶׁלוֹ, יְצוֹרְפוּ נָא אִמְרֵי פִי וְהֶגְיוֹן לִבִּי לַתְּפִילּוֹת כָּל יִשְׂרָאֵל, וְיִהְיוּ לְרָצוֹן לְפָנֶיךָ יְיָ צוּרִי וְגוֹאֲלִי.

⁓ SHMA ⁓

Recite this entire section twice a day: morning (*shacharit*) and evening (*ma'ariv*).
If you wear *tzitziyot* during shacharit, take all four in your left hand and hold them near your heart.

If a minyan is not present, say:

אֵל מֶלֶךְ נֶאֱמָן:

DEUTERONOMY 6:4

COVER THE EYES. ALOUD IN UNISON:

שְׁמַע יִשְׂרָאֵל יְיָ אֱלֹהֵינוּ יְיָ | אֶחָד:

QUIETLY:

בָּרוּךְ שֵׁם כְּבוֹד מַלְכוּתוֹ לְעוֹלָם וָעֶד:

DEUTERONOMY 6:5–9

If you are wearing tefillin: Touch the arm tefillin as you say, "Fasten them to your hand as a sign." Touch the head tefillin as you say, "Let them be ornaments between your eyes." Kiss your fingertips.

LOVE the LORD, your God, with all your heart, with all your soul, and with all your might. Let these words that I command you today be on your heart. Teach them repeatedly to your children, and speak of them when you sit in your home, when you walk on the road, when you lie down, and when you arise. Fasten them to your hand as a sign, and let them be ornaments between your eyes. Write them upon the doorposts of your home and on your gates.

DEUTERONOMY 11:13–21

IF YOU dutifully heed my commandments that I command you today, to love the LORD your God and to serve him with all your heart and with all your soul, then I will provide rain for your land in its time: the autumn rain and the spring rain. You will gather in your grain, your fresh wine, and your fine oil. And I will provide grass in your fields for your cattle, and you will eat and be satisfied.

Guard yourselves, or else your hearts will be seduced, and you will stray and serve other gods and bow in worship to them. Then the LORD's anger will flare up against you. He will seal off heaven so there will be no rain, and the ground will not give you its harvest. You will quickly perish from the good land that the LORD is giving you.

If you are wearing tefillin: Touch the arm tefillin as you say, "Fasten them to your hand as a sign." Touch the head tefillin as you say, "Let them be ornaments between your eyes." Kiss your fingertips.

So place these words of mine upon your heart and upon your soul. Fasten them to your hand as a sign, and let them be ornaments between your eyes. Teach them to your children, speaking of them when you sit in your home, when you walk on the road, when you lie down, and when you arise. Write them upon the doorposts of your home and on your gates. Do this so that your days and the days of your children may be abundant upon the ground that the LORD swore to give to your fathers for as long as heaven is above the earth.

If you are wearing tefillin: Touch the arm tefillin as you say, "Fasten them to your hand as a sign."
Touch the head tefillin as you say, "Let them be ornaments between your eyes." Kiss your fingertips.

וְאָהַבְתָּ אֵת יְיָ אֱלֹהֶיךָ, בְּכָל־לְבָבְךָ וּבְכָל־נַפְשְׁךָ, וּבְכָל־מְאֹדֶךָ: וְהָיוּ הַדְּבָרִים הָאֵלֶּה, אֲשֶׁר אָנֹכִי מְצַוְּךָ הַיּוֹם, עַל־לְבָבֶךָ: וְשִׁנַּנְתָּם לְבָנֶיךָ, וְדִבַּרְתָּ בָּם, בְּשִׁבְתְּךָ בְּבֵיתֶךָ, וּבְלֶכְתְּךָ בַדֶּרֶךְ, וּבְשָׁכְבְּךָ וּבְקוּמֶךָ: וּקְשַׁרְתָּם לְאוֹת עַל־יָדֶךָ, וְהָיוּ לְטֹטָפֹת בֵּין עֵינֶיךָ: וּכְתַבְתָּם עַל־מְזוּזֹת בֵּיתֶךָ, וּבִשְׁעָרֶיךָ:

וְהָיָה אִם־שָׁמֹעַ תִּשְׁמְעוּ אֶל־מִצְוֹתַי, אֲשֶׁר אָנֹכִי מְצַוֶּה אֶתְכֶם הַיּוֹם, לְאַהֲבָה אֶת־יְיָ אֱלֹהֵיכֶם וּלְעָבְדוֹ, בְּכָל־לְבַבְכֶם וּבְכָל־נַפְשְׁכֶם: וְנָתַתִּי מְטַר־אַרְצְכֶם בְּעִתּוֹ יוֹרֶה וּמַלְקוֹשׁ, וְאָסַפְתָּ דְגָנֶךָ, וְתִירֹשְׁךָ וְיִצְהָרֶךָ: וְנָתַתִּי עֵשֶׂב בְּשָׂדְךָ לִבְהֶמְתֶּךָ, וְאָכַלְתָּ וְשָׂבָעְתָּ:

הִשָּׁמְרוּ לָכֶם, פֶּן יִפְתֶּה לְבַבְכֶם, וְסַרְתֶּם וַעֲבַדְתֶּם אֱלֹהִים אֲחֵרִים, וְהִשְׁתַּחֲוִיתֶם לָהֶם: וְחָרָה אַף־יְיָ בָּכֶם, וְעָצַר אֶת־הַשָּׁמַיִם וְלֹא־יִהְיֶה מָטָר, וְהָאֲדָמָה לֹא תִתֵּן אֶת־יְבוּלָהּ, וַאֲבַדְתֶּם מְהֵרָה, מֵעַל הָאָרֶץ הַטֹּבָה, אֲשֶׁר יְיָ נֹתֵן לָכֶם:

If you are wearing tefillin: Touch the arm tefillin as you say, "Fasten them to your hand as a sign."
Touch the head tefillin as you say, "Let them be ornaments between your eyes." Kiss your fingertips.

וְשַׂמְתֶּם אֶת־דְּבָרַי אֵלֶּה, עַל־לְבַבְכֶם וְעַל־נַפְשְׁכֶם, וּקְשַׁרְתֶּם אֹתָם לְאוֹת עַל־יֶדְכֶם, וְהָיוּ לְטוֹטָפֹת בֵּין עֵינֵיכֶם: וְלִמַּדְתֶּם אֹתָם אֶת־בְּנֵיכֶם לְדַבֵּר בָּם, בְּשִׁבְתְּךָ בְּבֵיתֶךָ, וּבְלֶכְתְּךָ בַדֶּרֶךְ, וּבְשָׁכְבְּךָ וּבְקוּמֶךָ: וּכְתַבְתָּם עַל־מְזוּזוֹת בֵּיתֶךָ וּבִשְׁעָרֶיךָ: לְמַעַן יִרְבּוּ יְמֵיכֶם וִימֵי בְנֵיכֶם, עַל הָאֲדָמָה, אֲשֶׁר נִשְׁבַּע יְיָ לַאֲבֹתֵיכֶם לָתֵת לָהֶם, כִּימֵי הַשָּׁמַיִם עַל־הָאָרֶץ:

If you are wearing *tzitziyot*: Hold them with both hands. Kiss them each time you say the word "tzitzit."
Hold them in front of your eyes when you say "and you will see them."

THE LORD said to Moses, "Speak to the children of Israel and tell them to make for themselves a tzitzit on each of the corners of their garments throughout their generations. And they are to give the tzitzit of the corner a cord of *techelet*. It will be a tzitzit for you, and you will see them and remember all the LORD's commandments and carry them out. You must not explore after your heart or after your eyes, which lead you to act unfaithfully. Do this so that you remember and carry out all my commandments, and you will be holy for your God. I am the LORD your God who brought you out from the land of Egypt to be your God. I am the LORD your God."

AMIDAH

Recite this section each day at each of the three daily prayer times
(*shacharit*, *minchah*, and *ma'ariv*). Stand and face Jerusalem.

My Master, open my lips that my mouth may speak your praise![52]

PRAISE FOR THE PROMISES AND THE COVENANTS

Bow during this blessing:
Bend your knees when you see ▾.
Bend forward at the waist when you see ▶.
Straighten up when you see ▲.

▾**BLESSED** are ▶you, O ▲LORD, our God and God of our fathers, the God of Abraham, the God of Isaac, and the God of Jacob,[53] the great, powerful, and fearsome God,[54] God above all,[55] who is generous with kindness and owns all things, who remembers the devotion of the fathers and lovingly brings a redeemer to their descendants for his name's sake. King, helper, savior, and shield!

▾Blessed are ▶you, O ▲LORD, shield of Abraham.[56]

If you are wearing *tzitziyot*: Hold them with both hands. Kiss them each time you say the word "tzitzit."
Hold them in front of your eyes when you say "and you will see them."

וַיֹּ֣אמֶר יְיָ אֶל־מֹשֶׁ֥ה לֵּאמֹֽר: דַּבֵּ֞ר אֶל־בְּנֵ֤י יִשְׂרָאֵל֙ וְאָמַרְתָּ֣ אֲלֵהֶ֔ם
וְעָשׂ֨וּ לָהֶ֥ם צִיצִת֙* עַל־כַּנְפֵ֥י בִגְדֵיהֶ֖ם לְדֹרֹתָ֑ם וְנָֽתְנ֛וּ עַל־צִיצִ֥ת*
הַכָּנָ֖ף פְּתִ֥יל תְּכֵֽלֶת: וְהָיָ֣ה לָכֶם֮ לְצִיצִת֒* וּרְאִיתֶ֣ם אֹת֗וֹ וּזְכַרְתֶּם֙ אֶת־
כָּל־מִצְוֹ֣ת יְיָ֒ וַעֲשִׂיתֶ֖ם אֹתָ֑ם וְלֹֽא־תָת֜וּרוּ אַחֲרֵ֤י לְבַבְכֶם֙ וְאַחֲרֵ֣י עֵֽינֵיכֶ֔ם
אֲשֶׁר־אַתֶּ֥ם זֹנִ֖ים אַחֲרֵיהֶֽם: לְמַ֣עַן תִּזְכְּר֔וּ וַעֲשִׂיתֶ֖ם אֶת־כָּל־מִצְוֹתָ֑י
וִהְיִיתֶ֥ם קְדֹשִׁ֖ים לֵֽאלֹֽהֵיכֶֽם: אֲנִ֞י יְיָ אֱלֹֽהֵיכֶ֗ם אֲשֶׁ֨ר הוֹצֵ֤אתִי אֶתְכֶם֙
מֵאֶ֣רֶץ מִצְרַ֔יִם לִהְי֥וֹת לָכֶ֖ם לֵֽאלֹהִ֑ים אֲנִ֖י יְיָ אֱלֹֽהֵיכֶֽם:

AMIDAH

Recite this section each day at each of the three daily prayer times
(*shacharit*, *minchah*, and *ma'ariv*). Stand and face Jerusalem.

אֲדֹנָי שְׂפָתַי תִּפְתָּח, וּפִי יַגִּיד תְּהִלָּתֶֽךָ:

PRAISE FOR THE PROMISES AND THE COVENANT

Bow during this blessing:
Bend your knees when you see ▼.
Bend forward at the waist when you see ◄.
Straighten up when you see ▲.

▼בָּר֨וּךְ ◄אַתָּה ▲יְיָ אֱלֹהֵֽינוּ וֵאלֹהֵי אֲבוֹתֵֽינוּ, אֱלֹהֵי אַבְרָהָם, אֱלֹהֵי
יִצְחָק, וֵאלֹהֵי יַעֲקֹב, הָאֵל הַגָּדוֹל הַגִּבּוֹר וְהַנּוֹרָא, אֵל עֶלְיוֹן, גּוֹמֵל
חֲסָדִים טוֹבִים, וְקוֹנֵה הַכֹּל, וְזוֹכֵר חַסְדֵי אָבוֹת, וּמֵבִיא גוֹאֵל לִבְנֵי
בְנֵיהֶם לְמַֽעַן שְׁמוֹ בְּאַהֲבָה. מֶֽלֶךְ עוֹזֵר וּמוֹשִׁיעַ וּמָגֵן.

▼בָּרוּךְ ◄אַתָּה ▲יְיָ, מָגֵן אַבְרָהָם.

PRAISE FOR MIRACLES AND RESURRECTION

YOU are powerful forever, my Master. You resurrect the dead, fully able to save.[57]

In the summer, until December 4:	In the winter, until Passover:
He sends down the dew,	He causes the wind to blow and sends down the rain,

With devoted love he sustains those who are living; with deep compassion he resurrects the dead. He upholds those who fall,[58] heals the sick, sets captives free,[59] and maintains his faithfulness to those who sleep in the dust.[60] Who is like you, capable of powerful deeds, and who can compare with you? You are a king who causes death and resurrects,[61] and you make salvation sprout forth! You are faithful to resurrect the dead. Blessed are you, O LORD, who resurrects the dead.

PRAISE FOR THE HOLINESS OF GOD'S NAME

Recite this blessing during the private individual recitation of the *Amidah*.

YOU are holy, and your name is holy, and holy ones praise you every day. Selah. Blessed are you, O LORD, the holy God.

PROCLAMATION OF HOLINESS

Recite this blessing only during the cantor's repetition of the *Amidah* in a congregational setting.

FIRST CANTOR, THEN CONGREGATION:

WE WILL SANCTIFY your name in the world as it is sanctified in the highest heights. As it is written by your prophet, "And they were calling to one another,

ALOUD, IN UNISON:

Holy, holy, holy is the LORD of legions!
The fullness of the whole earth is his glory."[62]

Across from them they say, "Blessed!"

ALOUD, IN UNISON:

Blessed is the glory of the LORD from his place.[63]

PRAISE FOR MIRACLES AND RESURRECTION

אַתָּה גִּבּוֹר לְעוֹלָם אֲדֹנָי, מְחַיֵּה מֵתִים אַתָּה, רַב לְהוֹשִׁיעַ.

In the summer, until December 4:		In the winter, until Passover:
מַשִּׁיב הָרוּחַ וּמוֹרִיד הַגֶּשֶׁם.		מוֹרִיד הַטָּל.

מְכַלְכֵּל חַיִּים בְּחֶסֶד, מְחַיֵּה מֵתִים בְּרַחֲמִים רַבִּים, סוֹמֵךְ נוֹפְלִים,
וְרוֹפֵא חוֹלִים, וּמַתִּיר אֲסוּרִים, וּמְקַיֵּם אֱמוּנָתוֹ לִישֵׁנֵי עָפָר. מִי כָמוֹךָ
בַּעַל גְּבוּרוֹת, וּמִי דּוֹמֶה לָּךְ, מֶלֶךְ מֵמִית וּמְחַיֶּה וּמַצְמִיחַ יְשׁוּעָה.
וְנֶאֱמָן אַתָּה לְהַחֲיוֹת מֵתִים. בָּרוּךְ אַתָּה יְיָ, מְחַיֵּה הַמֵּתִים.

PRAISE FOR THE HOLINESS OF GOD'S NAME
Recite this blessing during the private individual recitation of the *Amidah*.

אַתָּה קָדוֹשׁ וְשִׁמְךָ קָדוֹשׁ, וּקְדוֹשִׁים בְּכָל יוֹם יְהַלְלוּךָ, סֶלָה. בָּרוּךְ
אַתָּה יְיָ, הָאֵל הַקָּדוֹשׁ.

PROCLAMATION OF HOLINESS
Recite this blessing only during the cantor's repetition of the *Amidah* in a congregational setting.

FIRST CANTOR, THEN CONGREGATION:

נְקַדֵּשׁ אֶת שִׁמְךָ בָּעוֹלָם, כְּשֵׁם שֶׁמַּקְדִּישִׁים אוֹתוֹ בִּשְׁמֵי מָרוֹם,
כַּכָּתוּב עַל יַד נְבִיאֶךָ, וְקָרָא זֶה אֶל זֶה וְאָמַר:

ALOUD, IN UNISON:

קָדוֹשׁ קָדוֹשׁ קָדוֹשׁ יְיָ צְבָאוֹת,
מְלֹא כָל הָאָרֶץ כְּבוֹדוֹ.

לְעֻמָּתָם בָּרוּךְ יֹאמֵרוּ.

ALOUD, IN UNISON:

בָּרוּךְ כְּבוֹד יְיָ מִמְּקוֹמוֹ.

And in your holy writings it is written,

ALOUD, IN UNISON:

> The LORD will reign forever—your God, O Zion—
> from generation to generation. Hallelujah![64]

In every generation we will tell of your greatness. From everlasting to everlasting we will sanctify your holiness. Our God, your praises will never, ever leave our mouths, for you are God, a great and holy king. Blessed are you, O LORD, the holy God.

THE HOLINESS OF THE SABBATH DAY

Recite this section only on the Sabbath: on Friday during *ma'ariv* and on Saturday during *shacharit, mussaf,* and *minchah.*

OUR GOD and God of our fathers, find favor in our rest. Sanctify us with your commandments, and give us our portion in your Torah. Satisfy us with your goodness,[65] and make us glad with your salvation. Cleanse our hearts, that they may truly serve you, and cause us to inherit your holy Sabbath, O LORD, our God, with love and favor, and may all Israel rest on it, who sanctify your name. Blessed are you, O LORD, who sanctifies the Sabbath.

On the Sabbath skip the blessings below and continue with "Thanksgiving for God's Goodness," page 148

PRAYER FOR DISCERNMENT

YOU bestow knowledge to humans and teach mortals discernment. Grant us knowledge, discernment, and understanding from you. Blessed are you, O LORD, who bestows knowledge.

PRAYER FOR REPENTANCE

RETURN us, our Father, to your Torah. Draw us near, our King, to your service, and help us to return to you in complete repentance. Blessed are you, O LORD, who desires repentance.

וּבְדִבְרֵי קָדְשְׁךָ כָּתוּב לֵאמֹר.

ALOUD, IN UNISON:

יִמְלֹךְ יְיָ לְעוֹלָם, אֱלֹהַיִךְ צִיּוֹן,
לְדֹר וָדֹר, הַלְלוּיָהּ.

לְדוֹר וָדוֹר נַגִּיד גָּדְלֶךָ, וּלְנֵצַח נְצָחִים קְדֻשָּׁתְךָ נַקְדִּישׁ, וְשִׁבְחֲךָ
אֱלֹהֵינוּ מִפִּינוּ לֹא יָמוּשׁ לְעוֹלָם וָעֶד, כִּי אֵל מֶלֶךְ גָּדוֹל וְקָדוֹשׁ
אָתָּה. בָּרוּךְ אַתָּה יְיָ, הָאֵל הַקָּדוֹשׁ.

THE HOLINESS OF THE SABBATH DAY

Recite this section only on the Sabbath: on Friday during *ma'ariv* and
on Saturday during *shacharit*, *mussaf*, and *minchah*.

אֱלֹהֵינוּ וֵאלֹהֵי אֲבוֹתֵינוּ, רְצֵה בִמְנוּחָתֵנוּ. קַדְּשֵׁנוּ בְּמִצְוֹתֶיךָ
וְתֵן חֶלְקֵנוּ בְּתוֹרָתֶךָ. שַׂבְּעֵנוּ מִטּוּבֶךָ, וְשַׂמְּחֵנוּ בִּישׁוּעָתֶךָ, וְטַהֵר
לִבֵּנוּ לְעָבְדְּךָ בֶּאֱמֶת, וְהַנְחִילֵנוּ יְיָ אֱלֹהֵינוּ בְּאַהֲבָה וּבְרָצוֹן שַׁבַּת
קָדְשֶׁךָ, וְיָנוּחוּ בוֹ יִשְׂרָאֵל מְקַדְּשֵׁי שְׁמֶךָ. בָּרוּךְ אַתָּה יְיָ, מְקַדֵּשׁ
הַשַּׁבָּת.

On the Sabbath skip the blessings below and continue with
"Thanksgiving for God's Goodness," page 149

PRAYER FOR DISCERNMENT

אַתָּה חוֹנֵן לְאָדָם דַּעַת, וּמְלַמֵּד לֶאֱנוֹשׁ בִּינָה. וְחָנֵּנוּ מֵאִתְּךָ דֵּעָה,
בִּינָה וְהַשְׂכֵּל. בָּרוּךְ אַתָּה יְיָ, חוֹנֵן הַדָּעַת.

PRAYER FOR REPENTANCE

הֲשִׁיבֵנוּ אָבִינוּ לְתוֹרָתֶךָ, וְקָרְבֵנוּ מַלְכֵּנוּ לַעֲבוֹדָתֶךָ, וְהַחֲזִירֵנוּ
בִּתְשׁוּבָה שְׁלֵמָה לְפָנֶיךָ. בָּרוּךְ אַתָּה יְיָ, הָרוֹצֶה בִּתְשׁוּבָה.

PRAYER FOR FORGIVENESS

FORGIVE us, our Father, for we have sinned. Pardon us, our King, for we have transgressed. For you pardon and forgive. Blessed are you, O LORD, abundantly gracious to forgive.

PRAYER FOR REDEMPTION

TAKE NOTE of our suffering, and take on our struggle, and quickly redeem us[66] for the sake of your name, because you are a strong redeemer. Blessed are you, O LORD, the redeemer of Israel.

PRAYER FOR HEALING

HEAL US, O LORD, and we will be healed; save us and we will be saved, for you are our praise.[67] Bring about complete healing for all our ailments.

For you, God and King, are a faithful and compassionate healer. Blessed are you, O LORD, healer of the sick among his people Israel.

PRAYER FOR THE HARVEST

BLESS this year for us, O LORD our God, and bless all its types of produce with goodness.

In the summer, until Sukkot:	In the winter, until Passover:
Send a blessing	Send dew and rain for a blessing

upon the face of the land. Satisfy us with your goodness, and bless this year as one of the best years. Blessed are you, O LORD, who blesses the years.

PRAYER FOR GATHERING OF THE EXILES

BLAST the great shofar for our freedom. Lift a banner to gather our exiles, and gather us together from the four corners of the earth.[68] Blessed are you, O LORD, who gathers those who are scattered of his people Israel.

PRAYER FOR FORGIVENESS

סְלַח לָנוּ אָבִינוּ כִּי חָטָאנוּ, מְחַל לָנוּ מַלְכֵּנוּ כִּי פָשָׁעְנוּ, כִּי מוֹחֵל וְסוֹלֵחַ אָתָּה. בָּרוּךְ אַתָּה יְיָ, חַנוּן הַמַּרְבֶּה לִסְלוֹחַ.

PRAYER FOR REDEMPTION

רְאֵה בְעָנְיֵנוּ, וְרִיבָה רִיבֵנוּ, וּגְאָלֵנוּ מְהֵרָה לְמַעַן שְׁמֶךָ, כִּי גּוֹאֵל חָזָק אָתָּה. בָּרוּךְ אַתָּה יְיָ, גּוֹאֵל יִשְׂרָאֵל.

PRAYER FOR HEALING

רְפָאֵנוּ יְיָ וְנֵרָפֵא, הוֹשִׁיעֵנוּ וְנִוָּשֵׁעָה, כִּי תְהִלָּתֵנוּ אָתָּה, וְהַעֲלֵה רְפוּאָה שְׁלֵמָה לְכָל מַכּוֹתֵינוּ. כִּי אֵל מֶלֶךְ רוֹפֵא נֶאֱמָן וְרַחֲמָן אָתָּה. בָּרוּךְ אַתָּה יְיָ, רוֹפֵא חוֹלֵי עַמּוֹ יִשְׂרָאֵל.

PRAYER FOR THE HARVEST

בָּרֵךְ עָלֵינוּ יְיָ אֱלֹהֵינוּ אֶת הַשָּׁנָה הַזֹּאת וְאֶת כָּל מִינֵי תְבוּאָתָהּ לְטוֹבָה,

In the summer, until Sukkot:	In the winter, until Passover:
וְתֶן בְּרָכָה	וְתֶן טַל וּמָטָר לִבְרָכָה

עַל פְּנֵי הָאֲדָמָה, וְשַׂבְּעֵנוּ מִטּוּבֶךָ, וּבָרֵךְ שְׁנָתֵנוּ כַּשָּׁנִים הַטּוֹבוֹת. בָּרוּךְ אַתָּה יְיָ, מְבָרֵךְ הַשָּׁנִים.

PRAYER FOR GATHERING OF THE EXILES

תְּקַע בְּשׁוֹפָר גָּדוֹל לְחֵרוּתֵנוּ, וְשָׂא נֵס לְקַבֵּץ גָּלְיוֹתֵינוּ, וְקַבְּצֵנוּ יַחַד מֵאַרְבַּע כַּנְפוֹת הָאָרֶץ. בָּרוּךְ אַתָּה יְיָ, מְקַבֵּץ נִדְחֵי עַמּוֹ יִשְׂרָאֵל.

PRAYER FOR JUSTICE

RESTORE our judges as at first and our counselors as in the beginning.[69] Take away our grief and groaning, and reign over us—you, O LORD, alone—with devotion and with compassion, vindicating us with justice. Blessed are you, O LORD, King who loves righteousness and justice.

PRAYER FOR THE PUNISHMENT OF THE WICKED

LET there be no hope for the slanderers, and may you instantly destroy all wickedness. Let all your enemies be swiftly cut down, and may you swiftly uproot, shatter, throw down, and humble the arrogant offenders, soon and during our lives. Blessed are you, O LORD, who smashes enemies and humbles the arrogant.

PRAYER FOR THE RIGHTEOUS

ON behalf of the righteous, the devout, and the elders of your people, the house of Israel, the scholars who remain, the righteous converts, and on our behalf may your compassion be incited, O LORD our God. Give a good reward to all those who truly trust in your name. Place our share with them forever so that we will not be put to shame, for we trust in you. Blessed are you, O LORD, the support and security for the righteous.

PRAYER FOR THE REBUILDING OF JERUSALEM

RETURN to Jerusalem, your city, with compassion, and dwell in its midst as you have said. Build it, soon and during our lives, as an eternal structure. And establish the throne of David within it. Blessed are you, O LORD, who builds Jerusalem.

PRAYER FOR THE RESTORATION OF DAVIDIC KINGSHIP

CAUSE THE BRANCH of David your servant to sprout forth swiftly, whose horn will be raised with your salvation, for we hope for your salvation all day long. Blessed are you, O LORD, who causes the horn of salvation to sprout forth.

PRAYER FOR JUSTICE

הָשִׁיבָה שׁוֹפְטֵינוּ כְּבָרִאשׁוֹנָה וְיוֹעֲצֵינוּ כְּבַתְּחִלָּה, וְהָסֵר מִמֶּנּוּ יָגוֹן וַאֲנָחָה, וּמְלוֹךְ עָלֵינוּ אַתָּה יְיָ לְבַדְּךָ בְּחֶסֶד וּבְרַחֲמִים, וְצַדְּקֵנוּ בַּמִּשְׁפָּט. בָּרוּךְ אַתָּה יְיָ, מֶלֶךְ אוֹהֵב צְדָקָה וּמִשְׁפָּט.

PRAYER FOR THE PUNISHMENT OF THE WICKED

וְלַמַּלְשִׁינִים אַל תְּהִי תִקְוָה, וְכָל הָרִשְׁעָה כְּרֶגַע תֹּאבֵד, וְכָל אֹיְבֶיךָ מְהֵרָה יִכָּרֵתוּ, וְהַזֵּדִים מְהֵרָה תְעַקֵּר וּתְשַׁבֵּר וּתְמַגֵּר וְתַכְנִיעַ בִּמְהֵרָה בְיָמֵינוּ. בָּרוּךְ אַתָּה יְיָ, שׁוֹבֵר אֹיְבִים וּמַכְנִיעַ זֵדִים.

PRAYER FOR THE RIGHTEOUS

עַל הַצַּדִּיקִים וְעַל הַחֲסִידִים וְעַל זִקְנֵי עַמְּךָ בֵּית יִשְׂרָאֵל, וְעַל פְּלֵיטַת סוֹפְרֵיהֶם, וְעַל גֵּרֵי הַצֶּדֶק וְעָלֵינוּ, יֶהֱמוּ רַחֲמֶיךָ יְיָ אֱלֹהֵינוּ, וְתֵן שָׂכָר טוֹב לְכָל הַבּוֹטְחִים בְּשִׁמְךָ בֶּאֱמֶת, וְשִׂים חֶלְקֵנוּ עִמָּהֶם לְעוֹלָם, וְלֹא נֵבוֹשׁ כִּי בְךָ בָּטָחְנוּ. בָּרוּךְ אַתָּה יְיָ, מִשְׁעָן וּמִבְטָח לַצַּדִּיקִים.

PRAYER FOR THE REBUILDING OF JERUSALEM

וְלִירוּשָׁלַיִם עִירְךָ בְּרַחֲמִים תָּשׁוּב, וְתִשְׁכּוֹן בְּתוֹכָהּ כַּאֲשֶׁר דִּבַּרְתָּ, וּבְנֵה אוֹתָהּ בְּקָרוֹב בְּיָמֵינוּ בִּנְיַן עוֹלָם, וְכִסֵּא דָוִד מְהֵרָה לְתוֹכָהּ תָּכִין. בָּרוּךְ אַתָּה יְיָ, בּוֹנֵה יְרוּשָׁלָיִם.

PRAYER FOR THE RESTORATION OF DAVIDIC KINGSHIP

אֶת צֶמַח דָּוִד עַבְדְּךָ מְהֵרָה תַצְמִיחַ, וְקַרְנוֹ תָּרוּם בִּישׁוּעָתֶךָ, כִּי לִישׁוּעָתְךָ קִוִּינוּ כָּל הַיּוֹם. בָּרוּךְ אַתָּה יְיָ, מַצְמִיחַ קֶרֶן יְשׁוּעָה.

PRAYER FOR ACCEPTANCE

HEAR our voice, O LORD our God. Take pity and have compassion on us, and accept our prayer with compassion and favor. Our King, do not turn us away from your presence empty handed! For you hear the prayer of every mouth. Blessed are you, O LORD, who hears prayer.

THANKSGIVING FOR THE TEMPLE SERVICE

SHOW favor to your people Israel and their prayer, O LORD, our God, and bring back the service to the inner chamber of your house. May you favorably accept the fire offerings of Israel and their loving prayer, and may the service of your people Israel always be favorable.

Let our eyes behold your compassionate return to Zion. Blessed are you, O LORD, who is bringing back his Dwelling Presence to Zion.

THANKSGIVING FOR GOD'S GOODNESS

Continue here on the Sabbath and on weekdays.
Bow during this blessing:
Bend your knees when you see ▼.
Bend forward at the waist when you see ▶.
Straighten up when you see ▲.

▼**WE ARE THANKFUL**[70] that you, ▲O LORD, are our God and God of our fathers forever and ever. You are the rock of our lives, the shield of our salvation[71] in every generation. We will give thanks to you and praise you[72] for our lives that are placed in your care, for our souls that are under your protection, for your miracles that are with us daily, and for your incomprehensible acts of goodness that happen all the time: evening, morning, and afternoon. We call you "good" because your compassions never stop and "compassionate" because your kindness never ends.[73] Since long ago we have hoped in you.[74]

For all these things, may your name be blessed and lifted up, our King, continually and forever and ever. Every living thing will acknowledge you. Selah. They will truly praise your name, the God of our salvation and our help. Selah.

▼Blessed are ▶you, O ▲LORD; "Good" is your name,[75] and it is fitting to thank you.

PRAYER FOR ACCEPTANCE

שְׁמַע קוֹלֵנוּ, יְיָ אֱלֹהֵינוּ, חוּס וְרַחֵם עָלֵינוּ, וְקַבֵּל בְּרַחֲמִים וּבְרָצוֹן אֶת תְּפִלָּתֵנוּ. וּמִלְּפָנֶיךָ מַלְכֵּנוּ, רֵיקָם אַל תְּשִׁיבֵנוּ. כִּי אַתָּה שׁוֹמֵעַ תְּפִלַּת כָּל פֶּה. בָּרוּךְ אַתָּה יְיָ, שׁוֹמֵעַ הַתְּפִלָּה.

THANKSGIVING FOR THE TEMPLE SERVICE

רְצֵה יְיָ אֱלֹהֵינוּ בְּעַמְּךָ יִשְׂרָאֵל וּבִתְפִלָּתָם, וְהָשֵׁב אֶת הָעֲבוֹדָה לִדְבִיר בֵּיתֶךָ. וְאִשֵּׁי יִשְׂרָאֵל וּתְפִלָּתָם בְּאַהֲבָה תְקַבֵּל בְּרָצוֹן, וּתְהִי לְרָצוֹן תָּמִיד עֲבוֹדַת יִשְׂרָאֵל עַמֶּךָ. וְתֶחֱזֶינָה עֵינֵינוּ בְּשׁוּבְךָ לְצִיּוֹן בְּרַחֲמִים. בָּרוּךְ אַתָּה יְיָ, הַמַּחֲזִיר שְׁכִינָתוֹ לְצִיּוֹן.

THANKSGIVING FOR GOD'S GOODNESS

Continue here on the Sabbath and on weekdays.
Bow during this blessing:
Bend your knees when you see ▾.
Bend forward at the waist when you see ◄.
Straighten up when you see ▲.

▾מוֹדִים אֲנַחְנוּ לָךְ, שָׁאַתָּה הוּא ▲יְיָ אֱלֹהֵינוּ וֵאלֹהֵי אֲבוֹתֵינוּ לְעוֹלָם וָעֶד. צוּר חַיֵּינוּ, מָגֵן יִשְׁעֵנוּ אַתָּה הוּא לְדוֹר וָדוֹר. נוֹדֶה לְּךָ וּנְסַפֵּר תְּהִלָּתֶךָ, עַל חַיֵּינוּ הַמְּסוּרִים בְּיָדֶךָ, וְעַל נִשְׁמוֹתֵינוּ הַפְּקוּדוֹת לָךְ, וְעַל נִסֶּיךָ שֶׁבְּכָל יוֹם עִמָּנוּ, וְעַל נִפְלְאוֹתֶיךָ וְטוֹבוֹתֶיךָ שֶׁבְּכָל עֵת, עֶרֶב וָבֹקֶר וְצָהֳרָיִם. הַטּוֹב כִּי לֹא כָלוּ רַחֲמֶיךָ, וְהַמְרַחֵם כִּי לֹא תַמּוּ חֲסָדֶיךָ, מֵעוֹלָם קִוִּינוּ לָךְ.

וְעַל כֻּלָּם יִתְבָּרַךְ וְיִתְרוֹמַם שִׁמְךָ מַלְכֵּנוּ תָּמִיד לְעוֹלָם וָעֶד. וְכֹל הַחַיִּים יוֹדוּךָ סֶלָה, וִיהַלְלוּ אֶת שִׁמְךָ בֶּאֱמֶת, הָאֵל יְשׁוּעָתֵנוּ וְעֶזְרָתֵנוּ סֶלָה.

▾בָּרוּךְ ◄אַתָּה ▲יְיָ, הַטּוֹב שִׁמְךָ וּלְךָ נָאֶה לְהוֹדוֹת.

THE PRIESTLY BLESSING

The cantor recites this blessing only during his repetition of the *Amidah* in a congregational setting.

CANTOR:

Our God and God of our fathers, bless us with the threefold blessing in the Torah, which was written by your servant Moses, pronounced by Aaron and his sons, the priests, your holy people, as it is said:

May the LORD bless you and protect you.[76]

CONGREGATION:

Let this be his will.

May the LORD shine his face upon you and be gracious to you.[77]

CONGREGATION:

Let this be his will.

May the LORD lift his face to you and grant peace to you.[78]

CONGREGATION:

Let this be his will.

THANKSGIVING FOR PEACE

PLACE peace, goodness, and blessing, grace, devotion, and compassion upon us and upon all Israel, your people. Bless us, our Father, all of us as one, with the light of your face. For by the light of your face you give us, O LORD our God, the Torah of life, devoted love, righteousness, blessing, compassion, life, and peace. It is good in your sight to bless your people Israel[79] in every moment and in every hour with your peace. Blessed are you, O LORD, who blesses his people Israel with peace.[80]

THE PRIESTLY BLESSING

The cantor recites this blessing only during his repetition of the Amidah *in a congregational setting.*

CANTOR:

אֱלֹהֵינוּ וֵאלֹהֵי אֲבוֹתֵינוּ, בָּרְכֵנוּ בַבְּרָכָה הַמְשֻׁלֶּשֶׁת בַּתּוֹרָה הַכְּתוּבָה עַל יְדֵי מֹשֶׁה עַבְדֶּךָ, הָאֲמוּרָה מִפִּי אַהֲרֹן וּבָנָיו, כֹּהֲנִים עַם קְדוֹשֶׁךָ, כָּאָמוּר.

יְבָרֶכְךָ יְיָ וְיִשְׁמְרֶךָ.

CONGREGATION:

כֵּן יְהִי רָצוֹן.

יָאֵר יְיָ פָּנָיו אֵלֶיךָ וִיחֻנֶּךָּ.

CONGREGATION:

כֵּן יְהִי רָצוֹן.

יִשָּׂא יְיָ פָּנָיו אֵלֶיךָ, וְיָשֵׂם לְךָ שָׁלוֹם.

CONGREGATION:

כֵּן יְהִי רָצוֹן.

THANKSGIVING FOR PEACE

שִׂים שָׁלוֹם, טוֹבָה וּבְרָכָה, חֵן וָחֶסֶד וְרַחֲמִים, עָלֵינוּ וְעַל כָּל יִשְׂרָאֵל עַמֶּךָ. בָּרְכֵנוּ, אָבִינוּ, כֻּלָּנוּ כְּאֶחָד בְּאוֹר פָּנֶיךָ, כִּי בְאוֹר פָּנֶיךָ נָתַתָּ לָּנוּ יְיָ אֱלֹהֵינוּ, תּוֹרַת חַיִּים וְאַהֲבַת חֶסֶד וּצְדָקָה וּבְרָכָה וְרַחֲמִים וְחַיִּים וְשָׁלוֹם. וְטוֹב בְּעֵינֶיךָ לְבָרֵךְ אֶת עַמְּךָ יִשְׂרָאֵל בְּכָל עֵת וּבְכָל שָׁעָה בִּשְׁלוֹמֶךָ. בָּרוּךְ אַתָּה יְיָ, הַמְבָרֵךְ אֶת עַמּוֹ יִשְׂרָאֵל בַּשָּׁלוֹם.

Recite this section each day at each of the three daily prayer times (*shacharit*, *minchah*, and *ma'ariv*).

OUR FATHER, WHO IS IN HEAVEN,

let your name be sanctified;

let your kingdom come;

let your will be done—

as in heaven, so on earth.

Give us today our bread of tomorrow,

and pardon our debts, as we also

have pardoned those indebted to us,

and do not let us be overcome by trials,

but rescue us from what is evil.

For yours is the kingdom and the power

and the majesty, forever and ever. Amen.[81]

For the sake of our Master Yeshua, in his merit and virtues, may
the sayings of my mouth and the meditation of my heart be
favorable before you, O LORD, my rock and my redeemer.[82]

Recite this section each day at each of the three daily prayer times (*shacharit*, *minchah*, and *ma'ariv*).

אָבִינוּ שֶׁבַּשָּׁמַיִם,

יִתְקַדֵּשׁ שְׁמֶךָ,

תָּבֹא מַלְכוּתֶךָ,

יֵעָשֶׂה רְצוֹנֶךָ,

כַּאֲשֶׁר בַּשָּׁמַיִם גַּם בָּאָרֶץ.

אֶת לַחְמֵנוּ לְמָחָר תֶּן לָנוּ הַיּוֹם,

וּמְחַל לָנוּ עַל חוֹבוֹתֵינוּ

כַּאֲשֶׁר מָחַלְנוּ גַּם אֲנַחְנוּ לְחַיָּבֵינוּ,

וְאַל תְּבִיאֵנוּ לִידֵי נִסָּיוֹן

כִּי אִם תַּצִּילֵנוּ מִן הָרָע.

כִּי לְךָ הַמַּמְלָכָה וְהַגְּבוּרָה

וְהַתִּפְאֶרֶת לְעוֹלְמֵי עוֹלָמִים. אָמֵן.

לְמַעַן יֵשׁוּעַ רַבֵּנוּ, בִּזְכוּת וּזְכֻיּוֹת שֶׁלּוֹ,

יִהְיוּ לְרָצוֹן אִמְרֵי פִי וְהֶגְיוֹן לִבִּי לְפָנֶיךָ, יְיָ צוּרִי וְגוֹאֲלִי.

PRAYER FOR THE RESTORATION OF ZION

Include this prayer as desired.

O LORD, in accordance with all your acts of righteousness, let your anger and wrath turn away from your city Jerusalem, your holy mountain.[83] Our Father, our King,[84] lift a banner to the peoples to return Israel to its pasture.[85] Gather us together from the four corners of the earth to our land,[86] and plant us within its borders[87] on the mountain of our inheritance.[88] Bring us to Zion, your city, with singing and to Jerusalem, your holy city, with eternal joy.[89] Build it in your compassion, and let it remain perched and inhabited in its place.[90] Establish your holy Temple in it,[91] and gladden us in your House of Prayer.[92] Return your Dwelling Presence to Zion, your city,[93] and send us Yeshua our Messiah a second time. Let him reign upon the throne of David in Jerusalem, your holy city. Lift up the horn of the salvations of your people Israel in the house of David your servant—salvation from our enemies and from the hand of all who hate us, just as you have spoken through your prophets.[94] O Lord, hear! O Lord, forgive! O Lord, listen and act! Do not delay, for your own sake, our God, for your name is called upon your city and upon your people.[95] Hurry, LORD, to help us![96] Ransom your people Israel from all its iniquities[97] and from all its troubles,[98] for the time to be gracious has come, for the appointed time has come.[99] Amen.

PRAYER FOR THE RESTORATION OF ZION

Include this prayer as desired.

אֲדֹנָי כְּכָל צִדְקֹתֶךָ, יָשָׁב נָא אַפְּךָ וַחֲמָתְךָ מֵעִירְךָ יְרוּשָׁלַיִם הַר
קָדְשֶׁךָ. אָבִינוּ מַלְכֵּנוּ, הָרֵם נֵס אֶל הָעַמִּים לְהָשִׁיב יִשְׂרָאֵל אֶל
נָוֵהוּ, וְקַבְּצֵנוּ יַחַד מֵאַרְבַּע כַּנְפוֹת הָאָרֶץ לְאַרְצֵנוּ, וְתִטָּעֵנוּ בִּגְבוּלֵנוּ
בְּהַר נַחֲלָתֵנוּ. וַהֲבִיאֵנוּ לְצִיּוֹן עִירְךָ בְּרִנָּה, וְלִירוּשָׁלַיִם עִיר קָדְשֶׁךָ
בְּשִׂמְחַת עוֹלָם. בְּנֵה אוֹתָהּ בְּרַחֲמֶיךָ, וְרָאֲמָה וְיָשְׁבָה תַחְתֶּיהָ,
וְכוֹנֵן בָּהּ בֵּית מִקְדָּשֶׁךָ, וְשַׂמְּחֵנוּ בְּבֵית תְּפִלָּתֶךָ. הָשֵׁב שְׁכִינָתְךָ
לְצִיּוֹן עִירֶךָ, וּשְׁלַח לָנוּ שֵׁנִית אֶת יֵשׁוּעַ מְשִׁיחֵנוּ, וּמָלַךְ עַל כִּסֵּא
דָוִד בִּירוּשָׁלַיִם עִיר קָדְשֶׁךָ. וְהָרֵם קֶרֶן יְשׁוּעוֹת עַמְּךָ יִשְׂרָאֵל בְּבֵית
דָּוִד עַבְדֶּךָ, יְשׁוּעָה מֵאֹיְבֵינוּ וּמִיַּד כָּל שֹׂנְאֵינוּ, כַּאֲשֶׁר דִּבַּרְתָּ בְּיַד
נְבִיאֶיךָ. אֲדֹנָי שְׁמָעָה, אֲדֹנָי סְלָחָה, אֲדֹנָי הַקְשִׁיבָה וַעֲשֵׂה. אַל
תְּאַחַר, לְמַעַנְךָ אֱלֹהֵינוּ כִּי שִׁמְךָ נִקְרָא עַל עִירְךָ וְעַל עַמֶּךָ. חוּשָׁה
יְיָ לְעֶזְרָתֵנוּ. פְּדֵה אֶת יִשְׂרָאֵל מִכֹּל עֲוֹנֹתָיו וּמִכֹּל צָרוֹתָיו, כִּי עֵת
לְחֶנְנָהּ, כִּי בָא מוֹעֵד. אָמֵן.

FOR FURTHER READING

Brown, Raymond E. "The Pater Noster as an Eschatological Prayer." *Theological Studies* 22 (1961): 175–208.

Donin, Hayim Halevy. *To Pray as a Jew: A Guide to the Prayer Book and the Synagogue Service*. New York, NY: Basic, 1991.

Elbogen, Ismar. *Jewish Liturgy: A Comprehensive History*. Philadelphia, PA: Jewish Publication Society, 1993.

Liebes, Yehudah. "Who Makes the Horn of Jesus to Flourish." *Immanuel* 21 (summer 1987): 55–67.

Munk, Rabbi Dr. Elie. *The World of Prayer*. 2 vols. Jerusalem, Israel: Feldheim, 2007.

Nulman, Macy. *The Encyclopedia of Jewish Prayer*. Lanham, MD: Rowman & Littlefield, 1993.

Rubin, Israel. *The How & Why of Jewish Prayer: A Guidebook for Men and Women*. Beit Shemesh, Israel: Arba Kanfot, 2011.

Sacks, Rabbi Sir Jonathan. *The Koren Siddur*. Jerusalem, Israel: Koren, 2009.

Scherman, Rabbi Nosson, and Rabbi Meir Zlotowitz. *Rabbinical Council of America Edition of the ArtScroll Siddur*. Brooklyn, NY: Mesorah, 2008.

Steinsaltz, Rabbi Adin. *A Guide to Jewish Prayer*. New York, NY: Schocken, 2002.

Young, Brad H. *The Jewish Background to the Lord's Prayer*. Tulsa, OK: Gospel Research Foundation, 2001.

Endnotes

1   b.*Shabbat* 127a.

2   b.*Ta'anit* 2a.

3   *Sifra*, Metzora 3:3.

4   b.*Brachot* 34b.

5   b.*Bava Batra* 116a.

6   Kevin Hanke, trans., *Die religiöse Denkweise der Chassidim*, unpublished translation from German, 139.

7   *Genesis Rabbah* 68:9.

8   b.*Yoma* 33a.

9   m.*Brachot* 5:1.

10   b.*Brachot* 9b.

11   b.*Ta'anit* 9a.

12   b.*Megillah* 23b.

13   b.*Brachot* 20b.

14   b.*Pesachim* 56a.

15   b.*Brachot* 61b.

16   *Genesis Rabbah* 44:12.

17   b.*Brachot* 17a.

18   m.*Brachot* 2:2.

19   b.*Megillah* 17b.

20   b.*Brachot* 28b.

21   b.*Megillah* 18a.

22   b.*Brachot* 32a.

23   b.*Megillah* 17b–18a.

24   b.*Sanhedrin* 97a.

25   Irenaeus, *Against Heresies* 5:33.

26   b.*Brachot* 28b.

27   b.*Shabbat* 10b.

28   m.*Brachot* 4:4.

29   t.*Brachot* 3:11; parallel in b.*Brachot* 29b.

30   m.*Brachot* 4:4.

31   b.*Brachot* 16b–17a.

32   m.*Sotah* 9:15.

33   b.*Ta'anit* 23b.

34   b.*Brachot* 12a.

35   *Pirkei Avot* 2:4.

36   t.*Brachot* 3:11; b.*Brachot* 29b.

37   Thomas P. Scheck, trans., *Commentary on Matthew*, The Fathers of
      the Church, vol. 117 (Washington DC: Catholic University of America
      Press, 2008), 88–89.

38   b.*Sotah* 48b.

39   Marie Ligouri Ewald, trans., *The Homilies of Saint Jerome*, vol. 1
      (Washington DC: Catholic University of America Press, 2001), 355–56.

40   b.*Gittin* 55b–56a.

41   b.*Bava Metzia* 30b.

42   b.*Rosh HaShanah* 17a; b.*Yoma* 23a, 87b; b.*Megillah*28a.

43   *Shulchan Aruch, Orach Chayim* 606:1.

44   *Sifra*, Bechukkotai 7:5.

45   *Pirkei Avot* 5:3.

46   b.*Sanhedrin* 107a.

47   b.*Brachot* 60b.

48   b.*Brachot* 16b.

49   b.*Kiddushin* 81b.

50   Paul Levertoff. *St. Matthew*, London, England: Thomas Murby & Co.
      (1940), 17.

51   *Didache* 16:5.

52   Psalm 51:17[15].

53   Exodus 3:15; 4:5.

54   Deuteronomy 10:17; Nehemiah 9:32.

55   Genesis 14:18–22; Psalm 78:35.

56   Genesis 15:1.

57   Isaiah 63:1.

58   Psalm 145:14.

59   Psalm 146:7.

60   Daniel 12:2.

61   1 Samuel 2:6.

62   Isaiah 6:3.

63   Ezekiel 3:12.

64   Psalm 146:10.

65   Jeremiah 31:13[14].

66	Psalm 119:153–154.
67	Jeremiah 17:14.
68	Isaiah 11:12.
69	Isaiah 1:26.
70	1 Chronicles 29:13.
71	Psalm 18:36[35]; 2 Samuel 22:36.
72	Psalm 79:13.
73	Lamentations 3:22.
74	Lamentations 3:25; Isaiah 25:9.
75	See Mark 10:18; Luke 18:19.
76	Numbers 6:24.
77	Numbers 6:25.
78	Numbers 6:26.
79	Numbers 24:1.
80	Psalm 29:11.
81	Matthew 6:9–14.
82	Psalm 19:15[14].
83	Daniel 9:16.
84	This is a common epithet for God in Jewish liturgy.
85	Jeremiah 50:19.
86	Weekday *Amidah* (Sephardic *nusach*); see Isaiah 11:12.
87	*Mussaf Amidah* for Shabbat.
88	Exodus 15:17.
89	*Mussaf Amidah* for festivals.
90	Zechariah 14:10.
91	*Mussaf Amidah* for festivals.
92	Monday *Slichot* for *Ta'anit Behab*; see Isaiah 56:7.
93	Introductory prayer before *Birkat Kohanim* on festivals.
94	Luke 1:69–71.
95	Daniel 9:19.
96	Psalm 38:23[22].
97	Psalm 130:8.
98	Psalm 25:22.
99	Psalm 102:14[13].